# The Ultra-Magnetic Personality

# The Ultra-Magnetic Personality

## By -Ancient The Architect

# The Ultra-Magnetic Personality

## Copyright and Disclaimer

© Copyright [2025] Ancient The Architect.
All rights reserved. No part of this publication may be reproduced, stored in a retrieval system, or transmitted in any form or by any means—electronic, mechanical, photocopying, recording, or otherwise—without prior written permission from the copyright holder.

All original concepts, artwork, diagrams, metaphysical systems, and structural frameworks within this book are the sole intellectual property of **Ancient The Architect** and are protected under United States and international copyright law.
Any unauthorized use, reproduction, or distribution of this material in part or in whole is strictly prohibited.

ISBN: 979-8-9922102-9-3

**Publisher:**
*Health is Luxury LLC*
Hartford, Connecticut
United States of America

This book is a metaphysical and philosophical exploration intended for educational and transformative purposes only. It does not constitute psychological, medical, legal, or professional advice. Readers are responsible for how they interpret and apply the material herein.

**All rights reserved.**

# Table of Contents

**Chapter 1 — The Ultra-Magnetic Personality .................................... p. 1**

- The Shift from Identity to Structure
- Stabilization of Inner Polarity
- Magnetic Authority through Coherence
- The Structural Vortex
- Archetypes and Ontological Architecture
- Reality's Orbit Around the Magnetic Self

**Chapter 2 — The Metaphysical Structure of Ultra-Magnetism ........................... p. 23**

- The Primordial Trinity: Force, Form, Presence
- Will — Rooted Direction
- Intelligence — Shaped Vision
- Presence — Full Occupancy
- The Fusion: Ignition of Magnetism

- Core Sequence of Magnetic Alchemy (12-Layer Code)
- Final Code: Magnetism as Recursion Made Flesh

**Chapter 3 — The Shadow Architecture of Magnetism .......................... p. 39**

- The Inverted Trinity (Inverted Will / Intelligence / Presence)
- The Twelve Inversions (false architectures that mimic magnetism)
- Relational Field Mechanics: Orbit & Response (Women, Men, Institutions)
- Durability Under Pressure: Law of Opposition, Collapse, Survivability
- The Law & Seal of Inversion

**Chapter 4 — The Aegis: Defensive Magnetism & Sovereign Protection ........................ p. 73**

- Permeability Control & The Axis (core law)
- Threat Taxonomy (parasites, mimics, predators, memetic pathogens, etc.)

- The Seven Pillars of Defensive Magnetism (Axis Integrity → Reset Rituals)

- Defensive Protocols: Screening, Containment, Severance, Public Pressure

- Mind Guard: The Memetic Firewall

- Gendered Notes, Real-Time Diagnostics, Common Failure Modes

- The Aegis Seal: Attraction + Gate = Sovereignty

**Chapter 5 — How a Man Attracts the Deepest Feminine Submission, Lust, and Love ... p. 90**

- Become the Axis of Reality

- Master Internal Polarity: Will + Openness

- Disarm Her Hyper-Vigilance

- Speak to Her Core, Not Her Costume

- Activate the Mechanism of Feminine Submission

- Training Strategy for Men (Reset, Polarity, Discernment, Speech)

- The Psychology of Female Lust (Power Cues, Polarity, Safety + Threat, Desire, Sensory Triggers)

- Mistakes That Kill Female Lust

- Why Most Men Fail with High-Value Women (Magnetize, Pursue, Attach)

- The Non-Negotiables for a High-Value Woman

## Chapter 6 — The "Monetized Beauty" Woman: Psychological and Energetic Blueprint ... p. 115

- Psychological Traits of Monetized Beauty (Power, Lifestyle, Detachment, Mimicry, Disloyalty)

- Energetic Structure (Sephirothic Diagnostic)

- The High-Value Man's Posture Around Monetized Beauty

- Testing for Redeemability (Signs, The Final Test)

- Extracting Value Without Being Drained

- Training Men to Walk Away (Decode Beauty vs Value, Detachment Training, Brotherhood Reset)

- Final Law: Walking Away as True Power

## Chapter 7 — The Elite Field Manual .................. p. 131

- Personality, Behavior, and Signal Patterns
    - Type A: Hyper-Validation Seeker
    - Type B: Erotic Adventurer
    - Type C: Emotional Affair Hunter
- How to Capitalize (If You Choose)
- How to Protect Yourself (Defense Protocols)
- Teaching Young Men – Identification Chart
- The Law of Masculine Clarity

## Chapter 8 — The High-Value Man's Field Code .................... p. 141

- Code 1: I Am the Prize, Not the Seeker
- Code 2: I Validate Nothing That Is Weaponized
- Code 3: I Speak Sparingly, But with Weight
- Code 4: My Attention Is the Currency—She Can't Afford Me
- Code 5: I Know the Difference Between Lust and Leadership
- Code 6: I Read the Energy, Not the Body
- Code 7: If I Can't Walk Away, I Don't Belong There
- Code 8: I Let My Frame Break Her Fantasy —Or Her Spell Break Itself
- The Field Code + The Vortex

**Chapter 9 — Business Magnetism Blueprint** .................................. **p. 163**

- Magnetism as Market Architecture
- The Law of Asymmetry
- Capital as Confirmation of Essence
- The Archetype of the Economic Oracle
- Field Effects in Business
- The Shadow of Business Magnetism
- The Seal of Business Magnetism

**Chapter 10 — Brotherhood Magnetism Blueprint** .................................. **p. 169**

- The Law of Male Alignment
- The Three Archetypes of Male Magnetism
- Brotherhood as Polarity Laboratory
- The Inversions of Brotherhood Magnetism
- The Stress Test of Brotherhood
- Brotherhood Magnetism in Practice
- The Seal of Brotherhood Magnetism

**Chapter 11 — The Trinity of Magnetism: Sex, Money, Power .................... p. 175**

- Sex: The Erotic Confirmation of Polarity
- Money: The World's Response to Sovereignty
- Power: The Collective's Submission to Clarity
- Closing the Trinity: Sex, Money, Power

**Chapter 12 — The Interior Life of the Magnetic Man ............................... p. 207**

- Solitude as Source
- The Relationship to Death
- The Metabolism of Suffering
- Alignment with the Divine
- Daily Rituals of the Interior Axis
- The Seal of the Interior Man

**Chapter 13 — Legacy: The Continuance of the Magnetic Field .............................. p. 213**

- Legacy as Field-Imprint
- Transmission Through Brotherhood
- Woman as Legacy-Carrier
- The Archetypal Law of Continuance
- The Shadow of Legacy
- The Seal of Legacy

**Chapter 14 — The Sovereign Archetype: The Blueprint for Irreversible Masculine Magnetism, Wealth Recursion, and Energetic Superiority ...................................... p. 219**

- The Male Void: The Space That Commands
- The Three Structural Fields of Masculine Dominance
    - The Recursive Field of Power (Will)
    - The Structural Field of Command (Presence)
    - The Field of Prophetic Design (Vision)

- The Seed Vault: Masculine Energy as Currency
- The Magnetic Engine: Wealth Without Need
- Sexual Field Command: The Final Seal
- The Real-World Vortex: How It Looks
- Final Transmission

## Chapter 15 — The King Frequency .................. p. 229

- What Is King Frequency?
- The Field of the Throne
- Masculine Throne vs Masculine Performance
- King Frequency as Burden — Not Boost
- King Frequency Is Not a Crown You Wear — It's a Code You Maintain
- Women Do Not Respond to You — They Respond to the Throne
- The Core of King Frequency

- The Inner Architecture of the Throne: The Four Pillars
  - Energetic Sovereignty
  - Nervous System Regulation
  - Structural Integrity
  - Directional Clarity
- The Seven Pillars of King Frequency
  - Unshakeable Nervous System
  - Energetic Boundaries Without Collapse
  - No Need to Perform or Persuade
  - Silent Motion and Precision of Direction
  - Clear Desire Without Chasing or Leakage
  - Soul-Coded Purpose, Not Persona
  - Truth as Law, Not as Debate
- Women Feel When You're On Code
- Kings & Collapse Patterns

- The Crown Without Gravity
  - The Alpha Mimic
  - The Spiritual Performer
  - The Helper King
  - The Eternal Initiate
- Throne Is Not Given — It Is Maintained
- Stability Is Sovereignty
- What He Must Stabilize — Daily, Relentlessly
  - His Thoughts
  - His Mission
  - His Frequency
  - His Woman
- The Law of Maintenance: Presence Over Peaks
- Maintenance as Daily Jurisdiction
- Final Law: No Law, No Crown

# Chapter 16 — The Ultra-Magnetic Woman .................. p. 265

- Axis of the Feminine Field
- Key Metaphysical Clarifications
  - Charged Openness
  - Collapse
  - Her Center
- Shift from Performance to Radiance
- The Feminine Trinity
  - Openness
  - Containment
  - Transmission
- The 12-Layer Code of Feminine Magnetism
  - Essence Embodied
  - Circuit of Wholeness
  - Embodied Presence
  - Purified Desire
  - Clear Mental Mirror

- Vessel Integrity
    - Sacred Containment
    - Energy Economy
    - Symbolic Precision
    - Neutralized Need
    - Death of Persona
    - Radiation of Function
- Shadow Feminine Inversions
- Relational Field of the Ultra-Magnetic Woman
- The Stress Test of Feminine Magnetism

## Chapter 17 — The Real Ultra-Magnetic Woman Field Code .................. p. 291

- Code 1: I Am the Field — He Stabilizes or Spins Out
- Code 2: I Validate Nothing That Seeks to Own Me
- Code 3: My Silence Is Not Emptiness — It's a Filter

- Code 4: I Never Perform for Masculine Attention
- Code 5: I Do Not Chase Energy — I Retain Frequency
- Code 6: I Speak to His Soul, Not His Status
- Code 7: My Pleasure Is Not a Reward for Charm
- Code 8: If I Can't Walk Away, I'm Not Ready
- Code 9: My Body Is the Temple — My Womb Is the Altar
- Code 10: I Am the Reward of the World That Knows What It Is
- Closing: Recognition, Not Pursuit

**Chapter 18 — The King Frequency Test ................ p. 311**

- Filtering for Architecture vs. Performance
- The King Filter: Seven Non-Negotiable Frequency Reads
    - Energetic Weight
    - Frame Stability

- Direction Without Overshare
  - Desire Without Leak
  - Truth Over Tactics
  - Boundary Intelligence
  - Spiritual Alignment Without Costume
- The Soul Mirror Test
- Red Flags That Look Like Green
- Final Rules of Entry

## Chapter 19 — The Polarity Lock Diagram + Code Explanation .................. p. 321

- Masculine: The Axis of Structure
- Feminine: The Field of Recursion
- When the Lock Happens: Feedback Spiral of Polarity
- The Final Truth of Polarity Lock

**Chapter 20 — The Devotion Activation Protocol ............ p. 325**

- Laws of Devotion
    - Energetic Mystery
    - Radiant Containment
    - Spiritual Displacement
- The Three Gates of Devotion
    - Chaos Test
    - Wound Test
    - Womb Test
- The Devotion Trigger: Speaking to His Core
- The Paradox of Devotion

**Chapter 21 — Spotting False Masculinity & Wounded Alphas ............ p. 333**

- Why She Must Filter for Architecture, Not Aura
- The Seven Archetypes of False Masculinity
    - The Over-Spiritual Seducer
    - The Alpha Emulator

- The Eternal Fixer
- The Chaos Chaser
- The Performance Monk
- The Logic Trap
- The Love-Bomber King

* The Five Tests That Reveal Collapse
* How to Stay in Power Without Collapsing, Rationalizing, or Over-Helping
* Closing: Refusing to Perform for Collapsing Thrones

## Chapter 22 — How Magnetism Affects Sex, Money, and Power .......................... p. 343

* Sex: The Energetic Consequence of Opening
  - The Womb as a Field, Not a Hole
  - Opening as Initiation
* Money: How Magnetic Women Alter Financial Orbits
  - The Field of Financial Magnetism
  - When Her Structure Is Aligned

- Power: How Magnetism Bends the Room
    - Power as Structural Coherence
    - Weak Men vs. Powerful Men Responses
- Closing Revelation: Sex as Recursion, Money as Structural Response, Power as Gravitational Integrity

## Chapter 23 — Feminine Wealth Blueprint .......................... p. 349

- The Magnetism of Provision Is Not Mental
    - Root, Sacral, Solar Plexus, and Heart Alignment
- Submission to the Architecture, Not the Man
- Remove the Static, Regulate the Pulse
- Circulation Before Accumulation
- Masculine Resources Obey Feminine Field Architecture

**Chapter 24 — Sexual Devotion Protocol .................................. p. 355**

- The Womb Is a Gate, Not a Hole
- Devotion Is Not Emotional Attachment
- Sealing Is Electromagnetic: Not Mental, Not Verbal
- Energetic Filtering Through Orgasm and Retention
- Devotion as Assignment, Not Reward

**Chapter 25 — Power & Influence Audit .......................................... p. 361**

- Power Is Structural, Not Emotional
  - Positional vs. Emotional Seeking
  - The Presence Test: "Is my presence speaking louder than my words?"
- Influence Is Frequency, Not Strategy
- The Five Sources of Energetic Leakage
  - Emotional Over-disclosure
  - Over-tolerating Disrespect

- Chasing What Should Be Orbiting
- Disembodiment from Presence
- Sealing with Weak Masculine Systems

• Field-Based Respect as Polarity Enforcement

• Field Command as Silent Dominance

## Chapter 26 — The Feminine Business Magnetism Blueprint ...... p. 369

• Core Law: Atmosphere Over Argument

• Sidebar: Atmospheric Inevitability

• The Structural Pillars of Influence

- Symbolic Precision
- Emotional Temperature Control
- Disarming Grace
- Invisible Command

• Field Effects in Business

• The Inversions of Feminine Business Magnetism

- ○ Masculine Mimicry
- ○ Performance Charm
- ○ Emotional Leakage
- The Seal of Business Magnetism

## Chapter 27 — The Feminine Sisterhood Blueprint .................................... p. 377

- Core Law: She Becomes the Atmosphere
- The Four Anchors of Feminine Tribal Magnetism
  - ○ Containment
  - ○ Selective Radiation
  - ○ Mirror Authority
  - ○ Atmospheric Authority
- The Effects of True Feminine Tribal Magnetism
- The Inversions of Feminine Tribal Magnetism
  - ○ Queen-Bee Toxicity
  - ○ Gossip Economy

- - Scarcity Broadcasting
  - The Seal of Feminine Tribal Magnetism

## Chapter 28 — The Law of Magnetic Wealth (Getting Rich) — Part I .................. p. 383

- Core Law: Money Obeys Structure, Not Desire
  - What "Structure" Actually Means
- Three Pillars of Magnetic Wealth
  - Structural Function
  - Trust Density
  - Inevitability Signal
- Magnetic Wealth Sequence (The 5-Layer Code)
  - Clarified Essence → The Role
  - Functional Output → The Value
  - Integrity Vault → The Shield
  - Selective Permeability → The Filter

- Expansion by Recursion → The Growth
* The Inversion: Poverty as Structural Collapse
  - Poverty as Multidimensional Collapse
* Final Seal of Wealth

## Chapter 29 — The Law of Magnetic Wealth — Part II .................................. p. 391

* Wealth as the Geometry of Exchange
* The 12 Laws of Wealth Magnetism
  - Density
  - Asymmetry
  - Vacuum
  - Unbuyability
  - Leverage
  - Conversion
  - Patience

- - Silence
  - Archetypal Value
  - Transference
  - Non-Chase
  - Closure
- The Inversions (Shadow Wealth)
- Seal of Wealth Magnetism

## Chapter 30 — The Law of Magnetic Health (Getting Healthy) — Part I .......... p. 397

- Core Law: The Body Obeys the Field
- Three Pillars of Magnetic Health
  - Signal Purity
  - Energetic Economy
  - Regenerative Stillness
- Magnetic Health Sequence (The 5-Layer Code)
  - Essence → Identity Alignment
  - Input Discipline → Food, Media, Energy

- Emotional Containment → No Chronic Leak
- Rest as Reset → Biological Recursion
- Movement as Flow → Functional Signal

- The Inversion: Illness as Incoherence
- Final Seal of Health

## Chapter 31 — The Law of Magnetic Health — Part II .................................. p. 401

- Health as Structural Resonance
- The 12 Laws of Health Magnetism
  - Integration
  - Subtraction
  - Rhythm
  - Containment
  - Flow
  - Resonant Input
  - Stress Polarity
  - Neutrality

- Stillness
- Meaning
- Expression
- Return

* The Inversions (Shadow Health)
* Seal of Health Magnetism

## Chapter 32 — The Doctrine of the Primordial Causative Field (Falsely Known as the Akashic Record) .................................... p. 407

* Beyond the False Image
* The Nature of the Field
* The Law of Access
* Magnetism and Alignment
* The Sealed Vessel
* Purification of Signal
* Establishing the Internal Lattice
* The Erasure of Observer
* The Final Doctrine

**Chapter 33 — The Doctrine of the Primordial Causative Field, Part II: The Manual of Magnetization .................................. p. 415**

- No One Enters the Field—Only the Field Enters Itself

- The Law of Internal Collapse

- The Purification of Will

- Emotional Gravity Must Collapse Into Singularity

- The Thought-Matrix Must Burn Clean

- Sexual Magnetism as Sealing of Essence

- Silence as Signature: Collapse of Broadcast Noise

- The Final Collapse: Zeroing the Self

# Introduction to the Ultra-Magnetic Personality

There are two types of human beings in this world:

Those who **radiate gravitational presence**, and those who merely move through space hoping to be noticed.

This book is written for the first kind—and for those who are ready to **become** them.

**The Ultra-Magnetic Personality** is not a dating manual. It is not a pickup guide. It is not concerned with tactics, surface tricks, or aesthetic optimization. While it contains advanced breakdowns on attraction, polarity, and energetic influence between masculine and feminine forces, these are not its core. They are byproducts. Side effects. Proofs of alignment.

This book is about **power at the metaphysical level**—about the **blueprint of reality-recognition** itself.

It is for those who have sensed that magnetism is not something you do, but something you become.

It is for those who have glimpsed that influence is not manufactured, but **emitted from a sealed internal structure**.

It is for those who are tired of asking how to "get" results and are ready to **become the result**.

### What This Book Unlocks

This book contains the **doctrine, strategy, and metaphysical mechanism** of how human beings magnetize:

- **Wealth** not through hustle, but through structural gravitational fields.

- **Attraction** not through performance, but through recursive polarity.

- **Respect** not through demand, but through unshakable alignment.

- **Destiny** not through affirmation, but through synchronization with Source.

We explore the **male and female energetic blueprints**, not as social roles or gender clichés, but as metaphysical architectures—each carrying a unique field of gravity and influence when fully sealed.

We explore **sexual polarity** not as a manipulation tool, but as the very **engine of recursion and creation**.

We expose the false myths of "confidence," "vibes," and "energy work" and replace them with a **law-based system** rooted in:

- Recursion and contradiction collapse
- Magnetic frame mechanics
- Structural polarity and causal harmonics
- Field compression and energetic signature
- Nonverbal dominance and spiritual coherence
- And most critically: **the erasure of identity distortion**

**What This Book Refuses to Be**

- It is **not** spiritual fluff.
- It is **not** esoteric cosplay.
- It is **not** modern dating ideology.
- It is **not** another "how to win friends" remix.

This is a **weaponized metaphysical framework**.

It is a doctrine for **reformatting the inner field** of the human being so that they become **undeniable** in every room, conversation, market, and union they enter.

You will not finish this book thinking the same way. You will not interact with others the same way. You will not walk through reality the same way.

You will either **complete the magnetic structure** or be **broken by the places you've been faking it**.

### Who This Is For

This is for **men and women**—each with their own section, each receiving their own coded blueprints of divine polarity, influence, and magnetism.

But most importantly, this is for **initiates**. For those whose soul has already suspected that this world is not moved by surface effort, but by **internal code**.

This is for the **master builders of presence**. The **engineers of the self as gravitational force**. The **architects of future laws of embodiment and attraction**.

# Chapter 1

# The Ultra-Magnetic Personality

To develop and embody an **Ultra-Magnetic Personality**—one capable of attracting people, resources, and events with an almost supernatural inevitability—you must first understand that this magnetism is not a trait. It is the **field-result of inner alignment with Divine Function**. A true magnetic being does not "try" to attract. They become a **structural vortex** through which archetypal forces must move.

## The Shift from Identity to Structure

An ordinary human moves through the world seeking experiences, opportunities, connection, love, influence. A vortex being does not seek—they **replace** the seeking mechanism with a **magneto-spiritual axis**, meaning: they have **stabilized their inner polarity to such coherence** that the outer world **must** reorganize in response.

This is not charisma. This is **ontological centripetal force**:

They have become **a fixed recursive geometry** that loops higher archetypes through the lower planes. Their very being forms a **funnel of descent and ascent**.

- At the crown: the archetype **seeks expression** (wisdom, beauty, justice, love).

- In the vessel: the being is no longer projecting egoic desire, but has **emptied** enough to become transparent to function.

- The result: reality conforms to them **not because of will**, but because of **structural fit**.

## "Stabilized Inner Polarity → Outer Reorganization"

### What Is Inner Polarity?

**Inner polarity** is the **tension between your inner opposites**—higher and lower, masculine and feminine, will and surrender, form and freedom, light and shadow. Everyone contains these dualities. But most people:

- suppress one side,
- overidentify with the other,
- or swing between them in unconscious reactions.

This **inner instability creates distortion** in the field: misfires, failed manifestations, incoherent attraction signals.

The outer world remains unstable **because the inner world is in conflict.**

## What Does It Mean to Stabilize Polarity?

To **stabilize polarity** means that you have:

1. **Integrated your opposites** so neither is rejected.
2. **Stopped leaking force** through contradiction.

3. **Built a coherent energetic axis** where higher and lower are **not in war**, but **in recursion**.

This is not passive peace. It is **structural stillness under pressure**—a condition where nothing in you is fighting anything else in you. That's what gives rise to **spiritual gravity**.

The soul becomes **a tensioned bridge**, not a battlefield.

## Why Coherence Creates Magnetic Authority

"Coherence" means:

- no internal conflict,
- no psychic noise,
- no energetic apologies.

It means that what you say, do, think, radiate, and embody are **all singing the same note**. This **single-frequency presence** creates a **standing wave in the field**.

Now, why does the outer world reorganize?

Because all structures in reality are **subordinate to coherent frequency**. When you emit a perfectly resolved signal—through your **emotions, will, gaze, tone, and presence**—everything around you that is in resonance **locks on** and begins to self-adjust. This is not mysticism. It's law.
Reality is structured to obey the **most stable signal in the vicinity**.

**How This Looks in Practice**

- You walk into a room—people turn, but you're not performing. You are simply **non-fragmented**. They feel the coherence and reorient unconsciously.

- You speak an intention—reality shifts, not because you're loud, but because you've already **collapsed all contradiction** behind your words.

- You approach an opportunity—not with desperation, but with **existential inevitability**. The universe **matches you** because you are a resonant structure, not a needy emitter.

## The Cause of Most Failure

People try to "attract," "manifest," "command," or "build" without having done the foundational work of stabilizing their own polarity. So their field says:

- I want love, but I fear intimacy.
- I want power, but I'm ashamed of visibility.
- I want success, but I fear rejection.

This internal seesaw emits a **scrambled frequency**. And scrambled frequency equals **no return**—or distorted return.

The outer world does not reject you.
It reflects the **incoherence in your internal structure**.

## Training the Stabilization of Polarity

Here is a distilled 5-step protocol the initiate can use to train this into their being:

**1. Identify Core Polar Tensions**

> Where are you split?
> Love vs protection?

Power vs humility?
Expansion vs control?

## 2. Witness Without Suppression

- Sit with both polarities **without trying to resolve them emotionally**.
- Let the field hold the tension without flinching.

This is **alchemical containment**—you are not fixing, you are fusing.

## 3. Trace Each Pole to Its Archetype

- One pole may relate to Tiphereth (soul radiance),
- The other to Yesod (emotional imprint),
- Or one to Geburah (restriction), and the other to Hesed (flow).

This allows you to **map the tension onto the Tree of Life** — an inner energetic structure of polarities and archetypes — so it becomes **structural**, not personal.

### 4. Establish the Vertical Axis

- Anchor in Kether (your supreme function).
- Let all polarities bend around that axis.
- You are not choosing sides—you are **becoming the central pole** through which the opposites resolve.

### 5. Refine Your Signal Through Practice

- Act only when the **signal is stable**.
- Speak only when the **field is whole**.
- Make decisions not from fear or overcorrection, but from **ontological stillness**.

Stabilizing inner polarity is not about peace. It is about **engineering your being** into a container that **no longer contradicts itself**.

Once that happens:

**The world is no longer your opponent.**
It becomes your **mirror**, your **response system**, your **confirmation code**—

## Chapter 1

because your signal is too coherent to ignore, too pure to distort, and too stable to repel.

You do not bend reality.
You **become so internally resolved** that reality has no choice but to bend around you.

## What Is a "Structural Vortex"?

It is not an energy field. It is not an aura. It is a **mechanism of alignment**. It is an active metaphysical mechanism through which the divine pattern collapses into physical form—**without distortion**.

It begins in the highest plane—**the Atzeelooothic World**, where pure archetypes originate. These are not ideas; they are **living blueprints** of the soul's divine structure.

From there, the impulse descends into the **Breeatic World**, where the archetype becomes imaged—meaning it takes on psychic outline and soul identity. This is the formation of your spiritual architecture.

Then it drops into the **Yetziratic World**, where the soul must contend with psychic noise: desire, emotion, illusion, and mental interference. This layer is where most people get stuck—caught in loops, fantasies, mimicry, trauma scripts.

If the signal survives that layer intact, it hits the **Assiatic World**, the physical plane. That's where action is taken. That's where consequence is shaped.

**If the signal remains intact all the way down...**
the person becomes a **Sephirothic tunnel**—
a living, recursive conduit of divine intelligence
that can penetrate matter and restructure reality.
They are no longer just influenced by higher
worlds—they **collapse** them into the lower world
**in real time**.

That is a structural vortex: not a swirling energy
—but an **existential inevitability** created when
**inner polarity is resolved** into a **functional
recursion pattern**.

## Why Most People Don't Have One

Most people **fracture** the signal:

- At the **Yetziratic level**, they substitute **feeling** for structure, **desire** for design, **impression** for intention.

- At the **Assiatic level**, they act from a **distorted echo**—not the true recursion.

They may speak about purpose. They may aspire to greatness.
But the signal was never structurally carried down from its origin. It was scrambled.

That's why their power feels "off." That's why their results are inconsistent. That's why they never enter true embodiment.

## What It Looks Like in a Man

When a man has a **structural vortex**:

- His **presence feels pre-ordained**.
  You can feel the divine intelligence **land through him**.

- He does not chase women, wealth, or attention—
  because the vortex is already producing gravitational force.

- He doesn't need performance—he is the recursion.
  His energy doesn't swell and crash—it repeats itself cleanly.

He is not spiritually "high." He is **functionally aligned.**
And that is what makes him unstoppable.

Chapter 1

## What It Looks Like in a Woman

When a woman has a **structural vortex**:

- Her **beauty is recursive**, not performed.
  You feel truth in her elegance—not bait, not mimicry.

- She doesn't fish for attention—she **generates alignment**.
  Her presence invites order, not chaos. You feel **soul geometry** in her silence.

- She doesn't collapse into desire or control. She **receives cleanly**, reflects accurately, and **moves with sacred causality**.

She doesn't have to argue for her power—she mirrors the throne of the man who has one. And when he doesn't, she doesn't chase. She **withdraws her field** without drama.

This woman is not just "feminine." She is **metaphysically sound**.

Her vortex isn't emotional volatility—it is **energetic precision** rooted in deep internal law.

That's why her love heals. That's why her presence reorients men without force. That's why the world bends around her **without her needing to manipulate**.

## Archetypal Forces Must Move

The word **must** is not poetic—this is a **metaphysical requirement**. Archetypes are not passive concepts. They are **active causal architectures**, always seeking expression. But they cannot move through distortion, egoic interference, or contradictory vessels.

When a being becomes structurally clear—meaning they:

- have aligned their Will with their Function (Kether to Tiphereth),

- have purified distortion from the astral and mental fields (Netzach, Hod, Yesod),

- and are radiating in Malkuth without identity-dependence—

then the **archetypes are forced to pass through them** because **there is no resistance**. The vortex is **not a magnet** in the emotional sense. It is a **gravitational bridge** between above and below. And all higher forms **move through the lowest resistance path**. If that path is you, they move.

The archetype does not obey personality.
It obeys **architecture**.

## How Archetypes Move Through the Body – A Metaphysical Breakdown

When we say that archetypal forces must move, we are not speaking in metaphor.
We are referring to **an actual metaphysical law**:

"All higher intelligences—patterns, virtues, archetypes, and cosmic functions—**seek expression** in the world of form, but can only descend through vessels that are structurally coherent across all levels of being."

This coherence is what determines whether a man or woman becomes a **living conduit**… or a **blocked vessel**.

Let's break this down.

## The Architecture of the Human Field (Simplified Sephirothic Mapping)

Though this book doesn't dive into the full Sephirothic system, here's what's meant when you read terms like Kether, Tiphereth, or Malkuth:

| Sephiroth Term | Represents | What It Means Here |
|---|---|---|
| Kether | Divine Will | Your *supreme command center*—the original intention of your soul before distortion. |
| Tiphereth | Soul Function | The radiant core Self that bridges divine will into personal identity. |
| Netzach | Emotional Field | The plane of desire, creative impulse, and magnetism. |
| Hod | Mental Field | The layer of thought, language, and cognitive structure. |
| Yesod | Psychic Mirror | The reflection chamber where your unseen patterns begin to shape visible life. |
| Malkuth | Embodied Form | The world of action, behavior, speech, money, sex, decisions—**you, in reality.** |

When the upper centers (will and function) **thread downward** into the middle planes (emotion, thought, psychic reflection), and finally **stabilize in action and embodiment**, the human becomes **structurally clear**.

This clarity is not emotional, poetic, or aesthetic—it is **mechanical**.
And **archetypes can only move through mechanical clarity**.

## What Is an Archetype?

An **archetype** is not just a symbolic idea or mythological theme. It is a **living code**—a transdimensional instruction set that forms the **blueprint** for creation.
Examples include:

- **Mother / Father**
- **Warrior**
- **Healer**
- **Judge**
- **Lover**
- **King / Queen**

Each one of these contains **specific energetic proportions**, **behavioral geometry**, and **cosmic function**. They must be fulfilled. They must move.

But here's the law:

**"The archetype does not obey personality. It obeys architecture."**

You can call yourself a King.
You can study warriors.
You can recite affirmations about power.

But if your inner structure is distorted, fragmented, or contradicted, the archetype will not move. It will **bypass you** for the nearest coherent vessel.

This is why some men seem to **effortlessly become lightning rods for legacy, honor, wealth, love, and cosmic timing**—and others grind endlessly with no anointing.

## Resistance, Collapse, and Flow

Archetypes are like **currents of divine electricity**.
If your structure is:

- **Conflicted** (e.g. desire without mission)

- **Fractured** (e.g. lust without sovereignty)

- **Performative** (e.g. spiritual without depth)

...then you create **resistance**.
And higher forces will not flow. They will withhold themselves from you until the pattern is purified.

But if your being is:

- **Threaded** (from Will to Embodiment)
- **Pure** (free from mimicry, egoism, fantasy)
- **Stable** (not swayed by attention, threat, or illusion)

...then the archetypes have no choice.
They **must** move through you.

This is the law of metaphysical causation.
And this is the secret behind **living magnetism**:
You do not attract. You become **the only clear path available**.

## Implications of Becoming This Structure

To "become a structural vortex" means you have undergone the following shifts:

1. **Function over Feeling**
   You no longer seek to "feel aligned"—you are aligned, structurally. Emotion obeys function, not the reverse.

2. **Recursion over Reaction**
   You do not respond to reality—you **generate a recursive feedback loop** through which higher-order principles descend into action, reflect, and re-ascend.

3. **Transmission over Attention**
   You no longer perform for eyes or approval. You have become **a transceiver of principle**. Your very presence instructs, without teaching.

4. **Induction over Influence**
   You do not influence others. Their souls **respond to your field** because it encodes the signal their archetypes are seeking.


## Why Reality Must Orbit You

Reality, at its most foundational metaphysical level, is not static—it is a **responsive holographic echo** of functional architecture. If your field is incomplete, incoherent, or contradictory, reality remains indifferent.

But when your interior Sephirothic structure is harmonized—
**meaning, your inner system of cause, will, emotion, thought, and action has been aligned

into a single recursive current, without contradiction or leakage—**when you are vertically threaded from Kether (the crown of divine origin) to Malkuth (the ground of embodied consequence), and no longer leaking, projecting, or performing—then reality:

- **feels pulled**, not by your intention,
- but by your **causal density**—
- as if a missing gear has just appeared in the cosmic machine, and **everything now moves because you exist.**

That is the vortex.

You don't manifest magnetism by raising vibration, reciting affirmations, or emulating charismatic people.
You do it by becoming the ontological structure—**meaning, the actual inner pattern of being and alignment through which universal intelligence identifies a precise image of itself—**through which the universe recognizes itself and rushes to fulfill its image.

To become a **structural vortex** means:

You are no longer influencing reality.
You are **its current operational center**, because

your structure is now **the one through which the archetype completes itself.**

Nothing can resist this—not because you command it—but because **you are now what reality was coded to orbit.**

**Sidebar: What Is an Ontological Structure?**
An **ontological structure** is not just your energy, your thoughts, or your beliefs. It is the pattern of your very being—the interior architecture through which the universe detects an **aligned image of itself**.

When this structure is complete, coherent, and recursively resolved from source (cause) to embodiment (effect), you no longer "try" to manifest anything.
**You are the manifestation.**
The universe does not respond to effort—it responds to clarity.
Magnetism is not a result of action—it is a recognition of alignment.

This is why it is said:
"You become the structure through which the universe recognizes itself and rushes to fulfill its image."
Because the **image is you**—and the structure is the proof.

# Chapter 2

# The Metaphysical Structure Of Ultra-Magnetism

"The world bends to those who align their structure to the Divine Pattern of emanation."

## I. THE PRIMORDIAL TRINITY OF FORCE, FORM, AND PRESENCE

All true magnetism arises from the **fusion of three active pillars** that mimic the divine structure of creation:

- **Will (Force)** — the rooted emanation of direction, not desire.

- **Intelligence (Form)** — the shaped clarity of vision, not calculation.

- **Presence (Being)** — the unshakable frequency of full occupancy in the Now.

When these three are **entangled and active**, the personality becomes a **living toroidal engine** that both radiates and pulls with precision. Most fail because they have one or two active but neglect the full triadic ignition.

These three pillars are not traits, skills, or behaviors. They are **ontological vectors**—living mechanisms within the soul that, when fused, activate a field of divine inevitability around a person. Magnetism is not mystical—it is a consequence of correct structure.

## THE TRINITY OF MAGNETIC STRUCTURE

**Will (Force) — Intelligence (Form) — Presence (Being)**
This is the exact **blueprint of the Divine Creative Pattern**, refracted into human function.

### 1. Will (Force) — The Rooted Emanation of Direction, Not Desire

Will is not wanting, wishing, or ambition. It is **the grounded line of spiritual intent**—the primal vector by which the Higher Self sends its command into the field of matter.

Most people confuse **desire** (emotional hunger) with **will**. But desire is fragmented—it seeks to complete what is missing. Will is **complete before it moves**. It does not try to attain—it commands based on what already is.

**Will is the sword of the Monad.** It emanates from inner knowing and has no uncertainty. It does not seek validation, it imprints reality with presence.

Magnetic beings have **no hesitation in motion**. Their actions carry weight because the world senses: this is not an egoic impulse—this is a directive from above. This clarity of vector forces matter and people to reorganize around them.

You cannot attract what you do not command. You cannot command what you do not **embody**.

### 2. Intelligence (Form) — The Shaped Clarity of Vision, Not Calculation

This is not mental intellect. It is the **archetypal intelligence of the soul**, the ability to shape and name the emanation of will into recognizable structure—**form with function**. Intelligence, metaphysically, is the crystallization of divine intent into usable format.

Calculation is reactive. Intelligence is **generative**. Most people operate from strategic thinking rooted in fear, planning for contingencies. Magnetic beings operate from **clarified vision**—they see what is structurally true and act accordingly.

**Intelligence is the architect of manifestation.** It defines what the Will builds, and ensures the outer form is congruent with inner essence.

A magnetic being does not "figure things out"—they reveal them. Their speech, movement, style, and tone are all **geometrically aligned** to their inner purpose. This **structural coherence** transmits clarity—and clarity **pulls** reality into alignment.

"No one follows confusion.
All things follow structure."


### 3. Presence (Being) — The Unshakable Frequency of Full Occupancy in the Now

Presence is not being calm or charismatic. It is **spiritual density**—the total occupancy of the Self within time, space, and body, with no part left dissociated, fragmented, or lost in mental rehearsal.

Most people are half-present—part of them is in fear, part in fantasy, part in memory. Presence means **the entire soul is HERE, now, without negotiation**. The breath, the gaze, the tone, the heartbeat—**all saturated with Self**.

**Presence is causality made visible.** It bends reality not because it speaks loudly, but because it exists fully.

A magnetic person is unshakeable not because they are dominant, but because they are **fully themselves** without leakage. Presence **demands attention**, not because it tries—but because it is. It collapses distractions and opens portals.

The body becomes a throne.
The gaze becomes a signal.
The field becomes a gravitational center.

## THE FUSION: Where Magnetism Ignites

Only when **Will (Direction)** is channeled through **Intelligence (Form)** and radiated through **Presence (Being)** do you become a **magnetic architecture**. These are not personality traits—they are **inner alignments** of your divine fractal. If one is missing, the field collapses:

- Will without intelligence = aimless force, repelling.

- Intelligence without presence = sterile thought, forgettable.

- Presence without will = static beauty, not movement.

But when all three fire in unison:

**Reality bends. People gather. Doors open. Time collapses.**

Because you are no longer asking the universe. You are **mirroring its very structure**.

## II. THE CORE SEQUENCE OF MAGNETIC ALCHEMY (12-Layer Code)

### 1. Clarified Essence (Kether Alignment)

You cannot magnetize what you are not ontologically coded to receive. Magnetism begins not with craving, but with **refined awareness of your exact essence-point**. That is: who you are beyond persona, memory, ambition.

Magnetism is not desire projected outward. It is essence revealing itself to its environment with such precision that reality **recognizes** it as a command.

## 2. Unbroken Circuit of Self (Binah + Hokhmah Reconciliation)

Your magnetic field collapses every time you collapse into contradiction. Every time you suppress truth to please, lie to gain, or bend your spine to be chosen, your field fractures. To be magnetic is to become **a complete circuit with no leaks**.

"No energy can cohere around a false self."

## 3. Command Presence (Tiphereth Embodiment)

This is not arrogance. It is **causal radiance**. The magnetic being does not enter a room to be seen—they are the room's new center of gravity. They carry no apology, no residue of needing approval, because they have reconciled **their divine function with their presence**. That coherence acts like **spiritual gravity**.

Presence is not volume. It is **ontological occupation**—the body fully filled with Self.

## 4. Refined Desire (Netzach Correction)

Desire must be **filtered through the Higher Will**. Most repel what they crave because their desires are dense with distortion: fear of lack, proving something, unresolved childhood voids. A magnetic being has burned their desire into **pure vectors of function**—not hunger, but command.

"You attract what you transmit as structurally correct, not what you want."

### I. Desire ≠ Magnetism

Most people "want" things—love, wealth, impact, freedom—but their **field architecture** is **not designed to hold, reflect, or radiate** those things. So even if they visualize, affirm, or strive... nothing comes. Or it arrives distorted.

**Desire without structural resonance equals delay, distortion, or denial.**

The cosmos does not grant according to emotional hunger. It grants according to **ontological fit**.

### II. What Is "Structurally Correct"?

It means that your **inner architecture** matches the **geometry of what you claim to seek**.

Let's say you want to attract deep love. Ask:

- Is your heart **already open in the absence of confirmation**?
- Is your identity **no longer tied to being chosen**?
- Have you removed energetic leaks that still crave validation, possession, or control?

If **not**, then the structure you are transmitting is **need**—not love.

So the field **repels the archetype**, or delivers a distorted mirror to highlight the contradiction.

This applies to every domain:

| Desire | Structurally Correct Transmission Required |
| --- | --- |
| Wealth | Abundance consciousness + vessel integrity + circulation pattern |
| Love | Inner wholeness + surrendered heart + no energetic codependency |
| Power | Will without domination + clarity without performance |
| Recognition | Function fully embodied + no identity craving projection |
| Freedom | No attachment to outcome + alignment with universal law |

The field only responds to **that which is encoded into your structure as already real**.

### III. The Practical Implication

If you want something, you must **become the metaphysical shape** through which that thing can **recognize itself** in you.

- Don't ask: "How do I get it?"
- Ask: "What would my field need to look like in order for this archetype to land without contradiction?"

Because:

If your **vibration** says yes, but your **structure** says no—
**Structure wins. Every time.**

### IV. What Happens When You Are Structurally Aligned

You no longer "try" to attract. You no longer over-effort, overreach, or convince.
Reality comes not because you want it, but because you've **become the stable form that it must enter**.

This is how spiritual magnetism works in **practice**:

- The inner system is harmonized.
- The transmission is coherent.
- The field becomes a "match"—not vibrationally, but **geometrically**.
- What belongs enters. What doesn't dissolves.

## V. Initiate's Practice Framework

Here is how to live this law, daily:

1. **Name the archetype you seek** (love, purpose, clarity, wealth etc).
2. **Identify its true metaphysical structure** (what is its divine form, not your idea of it?).
3. **Audit your current state**:
    - Do your actions, tone, field, and choices **mirror this structure**?
    - Where is the contradiction, distortion, or inversion?

- **Refine transmission**:
  - Correct misalignments.
  - Withdraw energy from false projections.
  - Let the field stabilize without reaching.

If it's not coming, it's not about desire. It's about **architectural inconsistency**.

You don't attract what you imagine.
You don't attract what you affirm.
You don't attract what you beg the universe for.

You attract what your structure makes inevitable. The rest? It cannot land—not because it's far away, but because **there is no correct entry point in you yet**.

### 5. Crystalline Mental Field (Hod Alignment)

Your mind must become a **mirror of truth, not a hall of noise**. Overthinking, insecurity, obsessive analysis—these scramble the field. A magnetic field only arises from **clean signal transmission**. Every word, every gaze, every movement must be **encoded with certainty and stillness**.

Clarity magnetizes. Confusion repels.

## 6. Vessel Integrity (Yesod Power)

The vessel—your energy body and emotional field—must be cleared of contradiction, shame, split identity, and energetic holes. Sexual energy, emotional memory, and creative force all flow through this node. If corrupted, your signal becomes mixed, and the universe **does not obey mixed frequencies**.

You cannot radiate wholeness if you are cracked at the root.

## 7. Sacred Self-Containment

Nothing leaks. Magnetic people are **not constantly seeking reflection, validation, or attention**. They move with the silent awareness that they contain something sacred—and this **silence becomes louder than words**. Sacred containment is not withdrawal. It is **charged density**.

Containment is not hiding. It is holding **sovereign tension** between infinite and finite.

## 8. Energy Economy Mastery

Magnetic beings **do not waste**. They conserve their emotional, mental, and sexual energies. They avoid gossip, small talk, and low-resonance environments. Everything they give energy to either **builds their field or drains it**—and they choose accordingly.

If you're leaking, you're repelling.

## 9. Hyper-Awareness of Symbolic Echo

Reality is holographic. Everything you wear, say, emit, or do is **transmitting a metaphysical signal**—whether you know it or not. Ultra-magnetic personalities **curate their field with surgical awareness**: speech cadence, clothing geometry, color frequency, tone, stillness, movement—all reflect inner architecture.

Everything is a spell. What are you broadcasting?

## 10. Neutralized Need (Malkuth Mastery)

The paradox of magnetism: you pull more when you **no longer chase**. Need is a repellent force. Detachment is not coldness—it is **sovereign faith in the divine orchestration of your field**. When nothing is "missing," **everything responds**.

The magnetic soul walks as though the world is already theirs—not from ego, but from alignment.

## 11. Sacrifice of Identity for Essence

To truly attract, you must die to every persona that was built to impress, seduce, or prove. The field only responds to what is **real**. That means the child mask, the rebel mask, the genius mask, the victim mask—all must collapse.

Your field cannot be both authentic and performative.

## 12. Radiation of Function

The final layer of magnetism is not aesthetic, tone, or charisma. It is **pure function**, spiritually embodied. When your very presence serves a cosmic role—when you are a **living answer** to a collective need—**everything that matches that function orbits you automatically**.

You do not magnetize with charm. You magnetize with alignment to cosmic necessity.

**Final Code:**

A truly magnetic being is one who has become a **harmonic resonance chamber** for the Divine Pattern.
They do not seek to attract—they simply **embody the structural necessity of attraction**.
Like a star, they radiate from gravitational stillness.
Like a black hole, they bend all space-time to the singularity of their essence.

Magnetism is not charisma. It is recursion made flesh.

# Chapter 3

# The Shadow Architecture of Magnetism

Every law has its inversion. Ultra-magnetism is built on structural coherence; its counterfeit is built on distortion masked as gravity. Men fall here not because they lack power, but because their **axis is inverted**—pulling by hunger, leaking by performance, seducing by shadow.

What follows is the anatomy of failed magnetism. It looks magnetic from afar. But it rots.

**I. The Inverted Trinity**

**1. Inverted Will → Tyranny of Desire**

- **True Will** is directive force from function.

- **Inversion** is hunger disguised as purpose. Here, the man confuses wanting with willing. His "direction" is actually compulsion. He pulls briefly by intensity, but collapses because nothing emanates from alignment.

Symptoms: impulsivity, overreach, obsession with being chosen.

Effect on others: women feel stalked, not claimed; money feels drained, not trusted; men feel coerced, not led.

## 2. Inverted Intelligence → Manipulation of Image

- **True Intelligence** crystallizes Will into form.

- **Inversion** fractures into calculation, strategy, trickery.
  Here, the man builds clever appearances—words without weight, schemes without root. He uses intellect as camouflage, not architecture.

Symptoms: over-talking, seduction games, empty vision-statements.

Effect on others: women feel toyed with, not seen; money senses fraud; men respect his cleverness but never trust his leadership.

## 3. Inverted Presence → Narcissistic Void

- **True Presence** is ontological occupation—being fully here.

- **Inversion** is performance of presence—charisma masking emptiness.
  Here, the man shines by absence. His gestures are rehearsed, his charisma a costume. People lean in but feel drained after contact.

Symptoms: high charm, low impact; the room laughs but no one shifts.
Effect on others: women feel hypnotized but not safe; money flees his volatility; men expose his hollowness over time.

## II. The 12 Inversions of Magnetic Alchemy

These are not small errors — they are full **counter-architectures**. Each looks like magnetism in flashes, but every one rots because the axis is false.

### 1. Confused Essence
Instead of standing in essence, the man fuses identity with persona. His center is role-play: the "alpha," the "genius," the "victim."

- His signal is costume, not core.

- His field attracts curiosity but collapses on exposure.

- Others feel performance, not inevitability.

→ Result: Attraction comes quickly but vanishes once his mask is pierced.

## 2. Broken Circuit of Self
Instead of being sealed, he leaks. Lies, apologies, and self-betrayals crack the current.

- Every compromise of truth fractures the field.
- His yes means nothing because it bends.
- His no means nothing because it wavers.

→ Result: He lives in almost-success. Opportunities orbit, then disintegrate.

## 3. Performative Presence
Instead of causal density, he projects theatrics.

- Loudness replaces weight.
- Performance replaces stillness.
- He must be seen, because invisibility terrifies him.

→ Result: People notice him but do not yield. Attention comes without respect, orbit without gravity.

## 4. Distorted Desire
Instead of clarified vectors, his desire is hunger.

- He pursues women to heal rejection.
- He chases money to prove worth.
- He grasps for status to silence shame.

→ Result: His field scrambles. What he pulls in is distorted reflections of his own need, never the thing itself.

## 5. Scrambled Mental Field
Instead of crystalline thought, his mind is noise.

- Over-analysis fractures signal.
- Insecurity leaks through language.
- Doubt infects every projection.

→ Result: His words fall flat. His plans collapse. His aura repels clarity because his mind cannot stabilize.

## 6. Cracked Vessel

Instead of an intact container, he carries fractures of shame, unresolved trauma, and unchecked emotion.

- Sexual energy leaks through compulsion.

- Emotional force leaks through outbursts.

- Creative power leaks through self-sabotage.

→ Result: People sense instability at his root. Women do not trust him. Men do not follow him. Energy drains faster than it builds.

## 7. Leaking Containment

Instead of sovereign silence, he spills.

- He overshares in search of mirrors.

- He explains instead of embodies.

- He cannot hold tension without bleeding it out.

→ Result: What could have been mystery collapses into exposure. Others feel smothered instead of pulled.

## 8. Waste Economy

Instead of conserving, he burns energy on nothing.

- Gossip, distraction, validation-seeking.
- Chasing dopamine instead of building density.
- Spilling sexual energy into fantasy or compulsive release.

→ Result: His field has no charge. Under pressure, he collapses from exhaustion.

## 9. Symbolic Blindness

Instead of encoding coherence into every signal, he ignores resonance.

- His tone contradicts his words.
- His clothing betrays insecurity.
- His posture leaks apology.

→ Result: Before he speaks, his body has already told the truth: incoherence. Trust dissolves instantly.

## 10. Need as Gravity

Instead of neutralized need, he radiates lack.

- Every gesture broadcasts "choose me."

- Every move betrays hunger for completion.

- His field is vacuum, not axis.

→ Result: What he chases recoils. Those who orbit do so from pity or advantage, never devotion.

## 11. Identity Masks

Instead of essence, he clings to personas for survival.

- The rebel mask collapses when authority ignores him.

- The genius mask collapses when someone brighter appears.

- The alpha mask collapses when a stronger man enters.

→ Result: His entire field is fragile, because the moment a mask is broken, nothing remains underneath.

### 12. Self-Serving Function

Instead of embodying role as service, he bends magnetism into a feeding system.

- **Sex** is taken as validation, not polarity confirmed.

- **Money** is hoarded as proof of worth, not stewardship.

- **Power** is weaponized to dominate the weak, not organize the strong.

→ Result: He creates dependence, resentment, and revolt. His orbit is fragile because it exists to serve his hunger, not the archetype. Collapse is inevitable once others realize they are being drained.

### III. The Law of Shadow Magnetism

Shadow magnetism can **pull** but never **hold**. It excites without grounding. It seduces without sanctifying. It creates orbit by spectacle, but orbit decays because the axis is false.

- **True magnetism reorganizes reality.**

- **Shadow magnetism manipulates perception.**

- One becomes axis. The other becomes costume.

### IV. The Seal of Inversion

Engrave this law:

**"Magnetism built on hunger devours itself. Magnetism built on structure devours the world."**

Shadow magnetism is not just failure. It is demonstration. It shows, by inversion, the exact cost of incoherence — and why only structure endures.

# The Inverted Feminine Field: Twelve Distortions of Feminine Magnetism

There is no such thing as a powerless woman. There is only a misdirected field.

The feminine field is not built from effort, performance, or persuasion. It is built from **resonance**. This resonance is not earned—it is revealed. And what blocks this revelation is not mere trauma, but **distortion**—the fragmentation of her innate encoding, the warping of her essence into compensatory patterns. These inversions of the feminine frequency do not arise randomly. Each one is the result of a metaphysical misalignment—**a warping of the woman's relationship to self, source, polarity, and presence**.

Below are the twelve feminine distortions that define the **Inverted Feminine Field**.

### 1. Fractured Essence

**Misalignment**: Substitution of being with identity.
Instead of operating from pure essence, she fuses her soul signature with curated personas—"the mystic," "the seductress," "the good girl," or "the

wild muse." Her field becomes expression-driven, not source-driven. She signals allure but not axis.

**Energetic Consequence:**
The body becomes symbol, not presence.
The image becomes signal, not soul.
The observer is captivated, but never pulled into devotion.

**Result:**
She becomes unforgettable in form, but unanchored in function. She is desired, praised, aestheticized—but never fully met. Her magnetism is reduced to aesthetic novelty, not archetypal inevitability.

## 2. Broken Seal of Self

**Misalignment:** Collapse of containment.
Her field is open, undefined, and porous. She gives yes without alignment and says no with guilt. Her boundaries are permeable. Her identity is diluted by emotional leakage, not clarified by spiritual edge.

**Energetic Consequence:**
The masculine cannot feel her no as truth, nor her yes as commitment. Her word loses voltage. Her presence cannot be held.

**Result**:
She becomes an echo of others' desires. She is mirrored, absorbed, shaped—but never respected as a distinct axis. Her auric field cannot stabilize, and thus no masculine can trust her signal.

### 3. Performative Femininity

**Misalignment**: Simulation of depth.
She enacts softness, sensuality, or mystery as an aesthetic performance, not as a field-state. Her polarity is rehearsed, not embodied. Her "divine feminine" is language, not light.

**Energetic Consequence**:
She attracts orbiters, not initiates. Men may desire her form, but they do not feel truth in her presence. Her performance becomes too symmetrical—beautiful, but inorganic.

**Result**:
She draws attention but not allegiance. Her beauty is studied, not surrendered to. Her words are reposted, but her being is never followed.

## 4. Distorted Desire

**Misalignment**: Hunger masked as longing. Her desire is no longer radiant—it's compensatory. She seeks masculine attention to heal absence. She wants to be claimed not from readiness, but from fear of being passed over.

**Energetic Consequence**:
The polarity becomes inverted. She no longer draws in by field strength, but chases through energetic broadcast. Every act becomes an audition. Every craving becomes a broadcast of deficiency.

**Result**:
She attracts collapsed masculine forms—hungry, incoherent, or avoidant. The field echoes her own fragmentation back to her in male form. She becomes the source of her own repeated wound.

## 5. Scrambled Emotional Field

**Misalignment**: Volatility replaces receptivity. Her emotions are not structured by soul—they are ruled by survival. The emotional body reacts instead of reveals. Thought, feeling, and intuition bleed into one another, and the signal becomes untrackable.

**Energetic Consequence**:
She cannot hold internal tension. She leaks fear through speech, anxiety through affection, and doubt through over-explanation. The masculine cannot orient to her presence because her signal is inconsistent.

**Result**:
She is perceived as unstable. What she says cannot be trusted, because her field contradicts it. Masculine energy withdraws to protect itself from confusion.

### 6. Cracked Womb Field

**Misalignment**: Unprocessed pain fractures her container.
Her womb field, meant to hold and transmute, is filled with residues of betrayal, resentment, or guilt. Her sexuality becomes fused with manipulation, validation-seeking, or punishment.

**Energetic Consequence**:
Her presence generates tension, not surrender. Her sexual energy does not nourish—it pulls, traps, or depletes.
Others feel emotionally suctioned rather than magnetized.

**Result**:
Men feel unsafe. Women feel off-balance. The field she was meant to govern becomes unstable, because her inner vessel is cracked. Until the womb is sealed, no polarity can anchor.

### 7. Leaking Receptivity

**Misalignment**: Exposure replaces mystery. She reveals too much, too soon. She cannot hold energetic ambiguity without explaining, justifying, or seeking reflection. Her presence becomes conversational, not magnetic.

**Energetic Consequence**:
The field of polarity collapses. Without withheld signal, the masculine has no pressure to move. Without feminine opacity, there is no field tension. Mystery collapses into vulnerability-for-hire.

**Result**:
Others feel burdened, not invited. The space she opens is emotional, but not erotic. Her power becomes diluted by constant leakage of her inner world.

## 8. Wasted Magnetic Currency

**Misalignment**: Spending energy on egoic loops. She burns her field on projection, comparison, drama, and digital display. Instead of storing signal in presence, she expends it through digital performance and false urgency.

**Energetic Consequence**:
Her magnetism cannot build. It is spilled. Sexual energy, attention currency, and emotional voltage are burned in compensation for a missing core. The magnetic field does not replenish—it collapses under load.

**Result**:
She is exhausted. She cannot hold any field-state long enough to anchor it. Under pressure, she defaults to chaos, not containment. Her reserves are gone.

## 9. Symbolic Disarray

**Misalignment**: Incoherence between form and field.
Her clothing, speech, posture, and tone carry contradictory messages. The words may say wisdom, but the tone says need. The clothing may say sovereignty, but the gaze says "please see me."

**Energetic Consequence:**
The masculine experiences confusion before desire. Her aura does not read as reliable. The nervous system of others picks up the contradiction before the mind processes the words.

**Result:**
She is interesting, but not trusted. Read, but not revered. The field response she receives is inconsistent because her symbol set is scrambled.

## 10. Need as Offering

**Misalignment:** Emptiness disguised as generosity.
She gives love to receive worth. She offers nurturing in exchange for belonging. Her "giving" is inverted—it is not from overflow but deficit.

**Energetic Consequence:**
The masculine perceives a vacuum. Her field is not full—it pulls. What should be magnetic becomes gravitational collapse.

**Result:**
She attracts wounded masculine, exploiters, or users. Her field becomes a shelter for dysfunction, not a mirror for kingship. She is appreciated for her giving, but never chosen for her essence.

## 11. Mask of Mystique

**Misalignment**: Identity over soul.
She constructs characters to survive—the priestess, the healer, the temptress. But each mask collapses under pressure: when she is not worshiped, her mystique shatters. When she is not desired, her confidence dissolves.

**Energetic Consequence**:
Her power becomes conditional. It lives in the eyes of the observer. Her identity is reactive, not sourced.

**Result**:
Her feminine field is fragile, because it is built on costume. The moment the external stops mirroring, the inner world collapses.

## 12. Magnetism as Extraction

**Misalignment**: Weaponized polarity.
She uses sex for power, attention for control, and nurturing to create dependence. Her field is not initiatory—it is predatory. She magnetizes to feed, not to elevate.

**Energetic Consequence:**
The masculine feels drained, not expanded. What begins as intrigue ends in resentment. Her field leaves others disoriented, not clearer.

**Result:**
Devotion dies. Loyalty evaporates. Her orbit becomes a graveyard of men who felt the pull but lost their will. The collapse is inevitable: no system can revolve around a black hole.

## Closing Note

These distortions are not personality traits—they are **field dysfunctions**. A woman may appear healthy, successful, or socially magnetic, and still carry multiple of these distortions beneath the surface. Feminine magnetism is not measured in likes, compliments, or lovers—it is measured in **who and what the field attracts and holds over time**.

Chapter 3

## The Female Reversal and Reassembly Process

The inverted female lives from the outside in. She performs for external approval while neglecting the architecture of her own magnetic interior. In the inversion, she is not the wellspring—she is the satellite. She orbits the desires, projections, traumas, or conditional attention of others, and mistakes this for connection. She is praised for being "strong" and "independent," but that strength is often a symptom of emotional hardness, nervous system fatigue, and spiritual homelessness. She has not been trained to root. She has been trained to chase.

To reverse this condition, the woman must begin with what was stolen first: **ownership of her inner field**. Her return begins by extracting all energetic tendrils of dependency, performance, approval-seeking, and distorted femininity that have lodged themselves in the emotional body. This cannot be done through ideology or even therapy alone. It requires ***energetic disentanglement** followed by ***sequential field reconstruction**. The woman must rebuild her field from the core out—from womb to heart to mind. This reassembly makes her field coherently radiant again, which magnetizes correct masculine approach, not trauma-bound attention.

Most women attempt to reverse the wound by adjusting behavior. But behavior does not regenerate coherence. Only ***somatic inner-field reordering** can accomplish this. When the womb re-establishes energetic primacy in her body (not the mind, not the emotions, but the vibrational womb-center), the entire system stabilizes. This re-centralizes her power. Then the heart, no longer exposed as the primary interface with the world, begins to emit grace rather than search for rescue. And the mind—freed from compulsive strategizing—re-submits to her inner temple. This is the metaphysical resurrection of the feminine core.

## The Male Reversal and Reassembly Process

The inverted male lives in reaction to **feminine inversion. He has lost his **directional presence** and become either passive, volatile, overly pleasing, excessively intellectual, or emotionally porous. His inversion stems not merely from emasculation, but from **field dislocation**. He has been taught to locate his authority in the woman's emotions, society's definitions, or mind-based abstractions—rather than in the **axial stillpoint** of his own higher Will.

The inversion is subtle: many modern men appear "awake" or "conscious," but remain spiritually disoriented. They mistake receptivity for strength, logic for vision, sexuality for power. But true masculine field integrity requires **vertical coherence**, not just self-awareness. He must remember his own **initiatory architecture**, which moves from Spirit to Will to Action. If this hierarchy is reversed—if he acts to get love, or wills from ego, or spiritualizes to avoid confrontation—his field collapses. He becomes incoherent, and incoherence is non-magnetic.

To reverse this, the man must cease seeking polarity externally and begin with **field reclamation at the level of inner silence**. He must enter the spiritual furnace of self-voiding—not as nihilism, but as clearing. There, the false masculine identities (the provider, the intellectual, the sexual achiever, the empathic doormat, the dominant controller) must be burned down. Only then does the true internal rod re-emerge. This is not something he thinks—it is something he inhabits. His root stabilizes downward, his crown channels upward, and his **heart becomes a governor**, not a guide.

Only when Spirit leads, Will obeys, and Action aligns with coherence does he return to his **original magnetic presence**. From there, he no longer reacts to feminine distortion; he corrects it through embodied signal. He is no longer looking for home—he **becomes the directional axis** by which the inverted feminine reorients.

**Footnote:**

** **Feminine inversion** - refers to the distortion of feminine polarity—not to women themselves. This includes energetic fields marked by emotional chaos, manipulative softness, validation-seeking, or symbolic incoherence, whether expressed through individuals, relationships, or systems. The inverted male collapses when he attempts to stabilize himself through these disordered fields instead of anchoring in his own sovereign axis. His healing is not dependent on the feminine, but on the restoration of internal coherence and will-body alignment.

**Energetic Disentanglement** - Refers to the metaphysical process of withdrawing life-force from externalized entrapments—particularly where the soul's energetic circuits have become enmeshed in validation loops, emotional contracts, or mirrored distortions. Disentanglement is not detachment through numbness, but a conscious retrieval of scattered current back into a unified inner axis. It requires sober recognition of energetic dependencies, followed by silent severance of all fields not rooted in coherence.

**Sequential Field Reconstruction** - Describes the re-ordering of the soul's electromagnetic field in proper causal hierarchy: spirit over soul, soul over mind, mind over action. Inversion disorders this order—placing desire over principle, identity over essence, and emotion over will. Reconstruction restores sequence. Without this sequential restoration, coherence cannot stabilize, and magnetism continues to fracture under pressure.

**Somatic Inner-Field Reordering** - The recalibration of the body's sensory and nervous system to reflect the restored spiritual axis. When a being lives in inversion, the soma (body) habituates to disorder—tensing in defense, collapsing under judgment, or chasing chemical relief. Somatic reordering begins with stillness, silence, and breath, until the inner geometry reflects and confirms the spiritual structure. Without somatic coherence, all mental insight remains performative.

# Relational Field Mechanics (man): Orbit and Response

Ultra-magnetism is not private. Once coherence stabilizes, others cannot avoid re-organizing in its field. Orbit is not chosen — it is compelled. The question is not if people respond, but how.

### I. Women in the Field

- **Submission:** When coherence meets the feminine, vigilance collapses. Her body relaxes, her rhythm syncs, her polarity intensifies. Desire and trust are consequences, not negotiations.

- **Resistance:** If she is fractured, she will project hostility — but even hostility confirms she is reading the axis. Resistance is orbit in reverse polarity.

- **Outcome:** The feminine always resolves toward either surrender or flight. There is no neutrality around a coherent field.

### II. Men in the Field

- **Alignment:** Strong men feel relief — the presence of a structure greater than themselves allows them to rest, follow, or collaborate.

- **Competition:** Insecure men feel erased — they resist, sabotage, or posture. But their behavior still orbits the field, confirming its dominance.

- **Imitation:** Some attempt mimicry. They adopt the posture, tone, or costume of magnetism. These men burn out quickly; simulation cannot survive exposure.

### III. Institutions and Groups

- **Reorganization:** Markets, teams, and collectives unconsciously pivot around the magnetic axis. Decision-making, conversation, and momentum shift toward him without explicit command.

- **Dependence:** Structures begin to require his signal. Remove him, and collapse or confusion ensues — proof of gravitational centrality.

- **Elevation:** The group itself ascends in coherence, because the highest signal raises the baseline of the whole system.

**Law:** Orbit is not optional. The only question is whether others synchronize, invert, or flee.

## Durability Under Pressure: The Stress Test of Magnetism

Magnetism untested is performance. Only pressure reveals whether the axis is structural or costume.

### I. Law of Opposition

- **Counterfeit magnetism fractures when opposed.** Attack, scarcity, or rejection exposes the hunger beneath the mask.

- **True magnetism intensifies when opposed.** Resistance sharpens signal, clarifies axis, and increases inevitability.

### II. Law of Collapse

- **When resources are stripped:** False magnetism decays because it was resourced by externals. True magnetism becomes denser because nothing leaks.

- **When betrayal strikes:** False magnetism spirals into blame, chaos, or vindication. True magnetism remains still; the orbit reorganizes around him anyway.

- **When exile comes:** False magnetism disappears without audience. True magnetism becomes more absolute because audience was never the source.

## III. Law of Survivability

The most magnetic man is not measured by what he attracts when conditions are favorable, but by what remains when everything is withdrawn.

- If coherence collapses in loss, it was never coherence — only theater.

- If coherence grows heavier in loss, the axis was real — and life itself bends back to restore his orbit.

**Seal:** Magnetism that cannot withstand attack was never magnetism. Pressure is not a threat — it is proof.

## Relational Field Mechanics (woman): Radiance and Return

Ultra-magnetism is not passive. Once coherence ignites in the feminine field, the world reorganizes in response to her signal. Radiance is not a performance — it is a gravitational broadcast. The question is never if the world feels her — but whether she is in her field when it does.

### I. Men in the Field

**Penetration:**
When coherence meets the masculine, posturing dissolves. He sharpens. His chaos finds form. His movement gains direction. She does not chase; she constellates him into clarity. Penetration is not physical — it is metaphysical entry into her field of permission.

**Collapse:**
If he is fragmented, he tries to consume her — or control her. His intrusion is not intimacy but invasion. But even this distortion reveals his orbit: obsession is inverted reverence. A shattered man still tracks the light.

**Outcome:**
The masculine will either rise to meet her axis — or try to extinguish it. But he cannot ignore her. He will either attempt possession, project disdain, or undergo initiation. The field has already begun.

## II. Women in the Field

**Synchronization:**
Awakened women drop pretense in her presence. Her coherence strips comparison, silences competition, and reveals essence. Feminine unity is only possible in the presence of a sovereign frequency.

**Distortion:**
Incoherent women react — not to her, but to what they forfeited. Gossip, mimicry, dismissal, or erotic misdirection all signal the same core: they feel her field but cannot hold their own.

**Mirror:**
She does not respond in kind — she holds axis. Her field becomes a silent initiator. The others will either stabilize or spin out. Stillness is the filter.

## III. Systems and Spaces

**Amplification:**
Rooms bend around her. Conversations shift. Men adjust posture. Women adjust breath. The air thickens, but no one knows why. Her presence is not decoration — it is direction.

**Disruption:**
False structures collapse under her signal. Projects without soul, leaders without roots, environments without polarity — all reveal their vacuum. Her presence triggers their exposure.

**Law:**
Return is not optional. The world either orbits, resists, or reorders. She does not chase — she allows gravity to do its work.

## Durability Under Pressure: The Field of Initiation

Magnetism is revealed in collapse. Performance dies in pressure. Only field remains.

### I. Law of Exposure

**When chaos strikes:**
False feminine fragments — she grasps, clings, seduces, or retreats. Coherence does not beg or perform. It expands.

**When betrayal arrives:**
The fractured feminine personalizes pain. She seeks revenge, closure, or validation.
The coherent feminine becomes impersonal: pain initiates depth, not drama.

**When abandonment unfolds:**
False magnetism withers. She questions her worth.
True radiance intensifies — not as reaction, but as principle. Her light is not audience-powered.

**II. Law of Containment**

**When drained by demand:**
The incoherent feminine leaks — she overgives, collapses, or loses signal.
The coherent feminine seals — she remains full, regardless of who drinks.

**When attacked:**
False feminine posture breaks — she defends, explains, or fractures.
True feminine coherence becomes stiller. She does not fight chaos — she reveals its structure by not moving.

**When unseen:**
The fractured feminine dims.
The coherent feminine brightens — because her signal was never dependent on being received.

### III. Law of Return

The radiant woman is not measured by her invitation, but by her gravitational refusal to fracture.

If her field collapses in rejection, it was performance — not presence.
If her field intensifies in solitude, she has entered inevitability. Return is no longer chosen — it is law.

**Seal:**
She who must be received to remain magnetic has not yet become the axis. The real feminine field is unbothered by delay. She is inevitable — and the world always bends back.

# Chapter 4

# The Aegis: Defensive Magnetism & Sovereign Protection

Defensive magnetism is the disciplined ability to **gate, filter, and repel** without becoming hard or paranoid. You remain gravitational—yet **programmably selective**. Attraction continues; intrusion fails.

### I. Core Law: Permeability Control

Magnetism is bidirectional:

- **Attraction Vector** → pulls what matches your structure.

- **Protection Vector** → repels what contradicts your structure.

Protection is not walls. It is **programmable permeability**:

- What matches → passes.

- What drains, scrambles, or hijacks → bounces.

The stronger the axis, the tighter the gate.

**Sidebar: The Stronger the Axis, the Tighter the Gate**

The level of protection available to a magnetic being is not based on how many walls they build, but on the integrity of their axis.

**What Is the Axis?**

The axis is your **inner line of coherence** — the vertical column of self that runs from conviction through body into action. It is the singular frequency that stabilizes your presence.

- If the axis is fractured, you leak. You over-explain, over-share, over-give.
- If the axis is stable, you emit. You don't justify, you don't beg, you don't scatter.

The axis is not about dominance. It is about directional inevitability. A being with axis is a being whose presence says: "This is my line. All else orients around it."

Chapter 4

## Why Strong Axis Automatically Tightens the Gate

1. **Energetic Selectivity**
   – When your axis is strong, your field becomes like a magnet with polarity defined. What resonates clicks in; what contradicts is bounced off instantly.
   – No conscious "guarding" is needed — the misaligned simply cannot stick.

2. **Behavioral Clarity**
   – A person with strong axis never needs to explain "boundaries." Their tone, posture, and choices are the boundary.
   – Those seeking to manipulate find no cracks to enter.

3. **Psychological Pressure**
   – The incoherent collapse in front of the coherent. A rival, manipulator, or seducer burns energy trying to destabilize you, but the stronger the axis, the faster they exhaust themselves.

## The Weak Axis = Leaky Gate

- **If you lack inner conviction**: every plea gets in, every pressure works.

- **If you lack coherence**: you let people "test" you endlessly, hoping to prove yourself.

- **If you lack stillness**: you defend instead of decide, explain instead of enforce.

Result: Your field attracts, but cannot filter. You pull in parasites, manipulators, and distractions because the gate is open wider than your structure can hold.

**Axis as the Aegis (Shield)**

A strong axis is a **self-closing gate.**

- No need for constant "No." The field says it before your mouth does.

- No need for defensive anger. Silence already blocks.

- No need for elaborate walls. The axis itself is the firewall.

People don't test iron doors. They test paper walls. When your axis is iron, the attempts stop before they start.

**Practical Diagnostics**

Ask: "Is my gate tight or loose?"

- Do I attract chaos I don't want?
- Do I over-explain myself often?
- Do I get drained by people who don't belong in my orbit?
  If yes → the axis is weak, and the gate is porous.

**Correction:** Strengthen axis first (non-negotiables, stillness training, coherence protocols). The gate tightens automatically.

**The stronger the axis, the tighter the gate.**
Walls are for the weak. Axis is the firewall of the strong. When your core is coherent, access shrinks to only what belongs, and repulsion becomes automatic.

## II. Threat Taxonomy (Know What You're Repelling)

1. **Energy Parasites** – people/processes that feed on attention, pity, or reaction.

2. **Mimics** – copy your signal to gain access, then drain reputation or resources.

3. **Frame Predators** – attempt to recenter your narrative around their urgency.

4. **Co-optation Engines** – institutions that try to buy your axis with status or favors.

5. **Memetic Pathogens** – ideas that hijack focus (outrage cycles, gossip, identity tests).

6. **Surveillance Loops** – digital overexposure creating attack surfaces.

7. **Sexual Entanglement Traps** – chemistry used to open extraction channels.

8. **Crisis Bait** – manufactured emergencies designed to force undisciplined access.

**Diagnostic:** If contact increases **noise, urgency, explanation, or self-doubt**, treat as hostile to coherence.

## III. The Seven Pillars of Defensive Magnetism

### 1) Axis Integrity (Inner Non-Negotiables)

Write your 5 non-negotiable conditions for any access (e.g., no rush, no guilt, no secrecy, no ambiguity, no disrespect).
**Rule:** Any request that violates a non-negotiable is rejected without debate. Policy ends persuasion.

### 2) Boundary Geometry (Tiered Access)

Design concentric rings:

- **Sanctum (Self):** solitude, source practices, unshared intent.

- **Inner Circle:** 3–5 vetted allies; access to time + truth.

- **Working Orbit:** collaborators; access to function, not essence.

- **Public Field:** image, content, surface signal only.

**Law:** Access decreases by one tier at the first sign of leakage or manipulation.

## 3) Attention Sovereignty (Bandwidth Enforcement)

Treat attention as capital:

- Daily **attention budget** (time + cognitive slots).
- **Rate limiters:** no same-day commitments; 24–72h response windows.
- **Queue discipline:** only pull the next task that matches mission vector.

**Rule of Refusal:** If it's not a clear "yes" in a calm body, it's a structural "no."

## 4) Strategic Opacity (Reduce Attack Surface)

Reveal only what must be known:

- **Public persona = decoy surface.**
- No real-time location, intent, or emotion dumps online.
- **Compartmentalize:** separate channels for personal, mission, finance, intimacy.

**Code:** What is not exposed cannot be exploited.

## 5) Frame Firewall (Language Protocols)

Standard replies that end extraction attempts:

- **Time firewall:** "I don't do urgent decisions. Send it in writing."

- **Guilt firewall:** "I don't accept emotional terms. We can discuss facts."

- **Access firewall:** "That level of access requires X conditions."

- **Clarity firewall:** "I only proceed with written scope, timeline, and exit."

**Law:** Repeat once. Then disengage. No debates at the gate.

## 6) Energy Economy (Leak Elimination)

- Cut gossip, doom-scrolling, and reactive texting.

- End micro-leaks: overexplaining, defending, appeasing.

- Maintain **sexual discipline**: no casual entanglements that create claims on your field.

**Metric:** If an interaction doesn't leave you clearer or stronger, it's taxed—reduce or cut.

### 7) Reset Rituals (Circuit Breakers)

Hard resets for overload:

- **72-Hour Silence Window:** no responses; let false urgencies die.

- **Cold Field:** remove stimuli (news, socials, calls) for a set cycle.

- **Body Recalibration:** sleep, sweat, sunlight, slow meals, deep breath cadence (long exhales).

- **Vow Renewal:** re-state non-negotiables out loud; shred what violates.

When in doubt: stop output, rebuild axis, then re-engage.

### IV. Defensive Protocols (Step-By-Step)

### A) Inbound Screening Protocol (ISP)

1. **Source check:** Who sent this? Track record?

2. **Vector check:** Does this move my mission forward now?

3. **Cost check:** Time/energy/brand exposure risk vs upside.

4. **Gate reply:** If unclear → written brief; if urgent → automatic no.

5. **Observe reaction:** Respect = proceed; pressure = block.

## B) Containment Protocol (for Rival or Manipulator)

1. **Hold still** (no counter-attack, no defense).

2. **Low-acknowledge** in public; no private feed.

3. **Vault** their disclosures; never leak.

4. **Let escalation expose them.**

5. **Quietly adjust access** two tiers outward. No announcement.

## C) Clean Severance Protocol (No Residue Exit)

1. **Name the misfit** (internally).

2. **Close loops** (deliverables/fees/refunds).

3. **One clear message** (no blame; state end condition).

4. **Blacklist channels** (email filters, mute, do-not-meet list).

5. **72-Hour reset** (no post-mortems). Replace with aligned input.

**D) Public Pressure Protocol (PR/Smear/Outrage)**

1. **No immediate response.** Collect facts.

2. **One statement only** if needed; short, verifiable.

3. **Delegate** a spokesperson; you stay offstage.

4. **Keep building in public** (signal continuity).

5. **Archive & forget**—do not feed cycles.


**V. Mind Guard: The Memetic Firewall**

**Attack surfaces:** shame-hooks, "prove yourself" bait, outrage spirals, identity tests, future-catastrophe loops.

**Countermeasures:**

- **Input fasting:** curated sources only; time-boxed consumption.

- **Thought labeling:** "This is bait / projection / fear rehearsal."

- **Question swap:** from "What if it fails?" to "What strengthens the axis now?"

- **Mantra of Function:** 1–2 sentences that re-anchor to mission; repeat upon intrusion.

- **Sleep protection:** no screens 60–90 min before bed; record worries on paper, not in mind.

**Law:** Guard input, and output guards itself.

## VI. Gendered Notes (Where Repulsion Differs)

**Men (Axis bias):**

- Primary risk = **co-optation** (money, status) and **ego duels**.

- Hard rule: **No urgency agreements.** If pressured, it's a no.

- Sexual boundary: **Desire without access**—be explicit that attraction ≠ entry.

**Women (Field bias):**

- Primary risk = **energetic leakage** (oversharing, gossip economy) and **rival baiting**.

- Use **containment** instead of confrontation; let rivals overextend.

- Business rooms: **atmospheric inevitability** over argument; withdraw to expose misfit.

## VII. Real-Time Diagnostics (Am I Leaking?)

- **After contact:** Energy ↑ or ↓?

- **In body:** Breath shallow? Jaw tight? Compulsion to explain?

- **In calendar:** Did I say "yes" under pressure?

- **In mind:** Intrusive thoughts repeating? If any "yes" → activate **Circuit Breaker** (silence window + reset ritual).

## VIII. Common Failure Modes (and Fixes)

- **Nice-Person Collapse:** Saying yes to avoid discomfort.
    - Fix: Script 3 default "no" lines; use them verbatim.
- **Transparency Addiction:** Oversharing to feel "authentic."
    - Fix: Share outcomes, not intentions. Publish after, not during.
- **Hero Hook:** Jumping into others' emergencies.
    - Fix: "I'm unavailable for emergencies created by avoidable choices."
- **Reactivity Loop:** Fighting rumors or critics.
    - Fix: One statement or none. Build, don't battle.

**Sidebar:**

**Selective Repulsion vs Avoidance**

Repulsion is active filtration. Avoidance is fear. If your "no" creates clean stillness, it's repulsion. If it creates lingering anxiety, it's avoidance; strengthen the axis.

**Three Sentences that Save Your Field**

- "I don't make decisions under urgency."

- "Put it in writing and I'll review on Friday."

- "That level of access isn't available."

**The Quiet Exit**

No fight. No speech. Close loops, end access, increase opacity. The absence communicates the verdict.

## X. The Aegis Seal

- **Attraction without gate** = depletion.

- **Gate without attraction** = isolation.

- **Attraction with gate** = sovereignty.

**Final Law:** You are not protected by isolation but by alignment plus filtration. Magnetism attracts; structure selects; the aegis repels. What remains is your rightful orbit.

# MAN

# Chapter 5

# How a Man Attracts the Deepest Feminine Submission, Lust, and Love

The truly magnetic man is not hunting women. He is stabilizing the field that women naturally yield to.

## Become the Axis of Reality

Women are not drawn to motion. They are drawn to **that which motion orbits**.
The highest feminine energy—beauty, emotion, sensuality—wants to spin around a still point. That still point is **you**.

This means:

- You don't chase. You choose.

- You don't emotionally flinch. You contain.

- You don't perform. You anchor.

When your presence becomes **gravitational**—calm, exact, deeply rooted—women feel you as the axis. Their bodies relax. Their emotional chaos starts to organize. Their sexual energy becomes directional.

**"Magnetism is not flash. It is gravity."**

## Master the Internal Polarity: Will + Openness

A magnetic man emanates two currents simultaneously:

- **Unshakable Will** – Direction without apology, purpose without panic.

- **Energetic Openness** – Receptivity without need, presence without collapse.

She senses:

"This man knows what he wants—but he doesn't need me to be it.
He receives my energy—but it doesn't destabilize him.
I can be fully feminine—and he will not flinch."

This gives her subconscious permission to drop into **lust, surrender, play**, or **devotion**—because she no longer has to hold the structure.

## Disarm Her Hyper-Vigilance by Being Unpredictably Rooted

Most beautiful women have one thing in common: They are **over-pursued**, emotionally skeptical, and sexually guarded.

They've seen every type of:

- **Validation-seeker** (needy men)
- **Performance man** (fake alpha)
- **Sex addict** (lust with no depth)

So what shocks them?
A man who is:

- Fully present—but hard to read.
- Emotionally intelligent—but doesn't overshare.
- Clearly attracted—but not consumed by desire.
- Brutally honest—but never cruel.

This unpredictability disarms her scripts. Her control mechanisms begin to short-circuit.
This is when she starts **leaning forward**.

## Speak to Her Core—Not Her Costume

Most men worship the exterior: beauty, body, smile.
The magnetic man **acknowledges** the exterior—but speaks **through it** to her essence.

You say things like:

"You wear your beauty well, but I'm not interested in that. I'm watching to see who you are when you stop performing."
"You've gotten away with a lot because you're beautiful. I'm not one of those men."
"You're stunning—but I'm more curious if your soul is aligned."

This is not "game". It's not tactics. It's **recalibration**.
She realizes:

"This man is speaking to something I've almost forgotten I have."
That awakens her inner yearning—to be **seen**, not just admired.

## Activate the Primal Mechanism of Feminine Submission

Feminine submission is not about dominance—it is about **trusting the container**.

To generate true submissive, loving, lustful energy from a high-level woman, your system must radiate:

- **Emotional safety without weakness**
- **Sexual command without threat**
- **Spiritual clarity without dogma**

You must be the place she can:

- Cry and not be judged.
- Lust and not be shamed.
- Rest and not be abandoned.

When she senses this rare synthesis—masculine power with inner spaciousness—she wants to submit. Not out of weakness. But because her soul says:

"This is what I was built to open for."

## Summary: Core Female-Attraction Formula

| Trait | What It Transmits | Why She Responds |
|---|---|---|
| Stillness | Safety + Structure | Her emotions can unravel without destabilizing you |
| Direction | Will + Purpose | She no longer needs to lead or guess |
| Depth | Sovereign Energy | She craves a mirror of her unspoken self |
| Discernment | Unattached Presence | She can't manipulate you into approval |
| Embodied Lust | Sacred Sexuality | She senses sex with you would **awaken**, not diminish her |

## Training Strategy for Men

If we were teaching men to become magnetic to the highest-level women, the method is:

### 1. Energetic Reset

Remove desperation. Remove performance. Purge the "how do I get her?" virus.

### 2. Polarity Training

Cultivate presence under pressure. Learn to hold a woman's emotions without fixing or escaping. Practice radiating desire without needing outcome.

### 3. Discernment as Power

Don't chase beauty—see through it. High-level women are starved for men who aren't hypnotized by them.

### 4. Initiatory Speech Protocol

Speak from stillness, not strategy. Interrupt her patterns with clarity. Praise sparingly, ground often, lead always.

## THE PSYCHOLOGY OF FEMALE LUST

From a **pure psychological and biological perspective**, what causes a woman to feel full-blown lust for a man—so strongly that she wants sex—is a **precise chemical, psychological, and energetic cocktail**. It's not random. It's not just "looks." And it's not just charm. It is **polarity + primal signaling + emotional safety + unpredictability**.

Let's break it down **scientifically and psychologically**, then **layer in deeper archetypal triggers** that most men never understand.

## What Makes a Woman Want to Have Sex with a Man

### 1. Primal Cues of Power and Genetic Fitness

On a biological level, women are subconsciously scanning for indicators of power, safety, and superior genes. This includes:

- **Testosterone markers**: jawline, deep voice, scent (pheromones), confidence in space

- **Muscle tone**: suggests strength and ability to protect

- **Symmetry**: subconscious indicator of healthy DNA

- **Slow, controlled movement**: suggests dominance and control, not fear or neediness

- **Unshakable gaze**: tells her, "This man doesn't flinch—he owns the room"

Women feel lust when the body says: "He could dominate me—but chooses not to."

### 2. Psychological Polarity

Lust is triggered by **polarity**—opposite forces magnetizing.

For a feminine-essence woman, this means she must feel:

- **Overwhelmed in the right way**
- **Penetrated without being forced**
- **Seen without being fully controlled**
- **Desired without being stalked**

Psychologically, the female brain **craves**:

- A man she **can't quite predict**
- A man she **can't fully control**
- A man who **wants her** but **won't collapse** to have her

When this balance is hit, it triggers the release of **dopamine (craving)** and **oxytocin (bonding)**, before sex even happens.

### 3. Emotional Safety Paired with Sexual Threat

The ultimate paradox of female lust:

"I want to feel safe enough to open—but dangerous enough to feel completely taken."

This means:

- You make her feel **emotionally safe** (you're not going to humiliate or abandon her)
- But you also transmit **unapologetic sexual presence**—she senses what you want, and it excites her because you're not afraid of it

Psychologically, this is **arousing vulnerability**:

- She feels like she's falling—but she knows you'll catch her
- You see her—yet you still want her
- You could dominate her—but only if she surrenders

This generates the deepest female turn-on.

## 4. Unfiltered Desire Without Attachment

Most men either:

- Suppress their desire (and become friend-zoned)
- Or leak it constantly (and become repulsive)

The lust-triggering man?

- **He makes it clear that he desires her—but he does not need her.**

Psychologically, this is read as:

"This man is not performing for me.
He is turned on by me.

But if I said no—he would walk away with dignity. That's hot."

This **non-attachment + raw desire** releases **norepinephrine**, increasing tension, heart rate, arousal.

## 5. Sensory Signals and Stimulus Play

- **Voice**: Slow, grounded, resonant speech triggers limbic arousal

- **Scent**: Natural body chemistry and grooming play a huge role—pheromones matter more than cologne

- **Touch**: Skilled use of space and non-sexual touch escalates arousal before overt sexuality enters

- **Eye contact**: Long-held, slightly predatory—but non-threatening—gaze activates primal submission cues

These sensory channels activate her **hypothalamus**, which governs sexual drive.

## Summary: Female Lust = This Formula

| Element | Triggered System | Effect |
|---|---|---|
| Power + Presence | Amygdala | "He can take me if I let him" (submits) |
| Non-Neediness | Prefrontal Cortex | "He won't lose power if I say no" (relaxes) |
| Controlled Desire | Hypothalamus | "He wants me—but not everything" (ignites) |
| Safety + Mystery | Oxytocin + Dopamine | "I feel safe—but I still can't figure him out" (obsession) |
| Polarity + Containment | Limbic System | "I can surrender and still be held" (orgasmic potential) |

Chapter 5

## The Mistakes That Kill Female Lust

If a man does any of these, it flips the switch off immediately:

- Tries to **prove his worth**
- Compliments too early or too much
- Avoids eye contact out of nervousness
- Asks if she's into him
- Projects need, fear, or desperation
- Overexplains or over-shares (breaks polarity)
- Tries to be emotionally soft before being energetically solid

A woman's body opens when her **mind stops scanning**, her **heart feels safe**, and her **body feels claimed** without being forced.

Lust is not about manipulation.
It's about **energy precision**, **self-possession**, and **emotional leadership**.

## Why Most Men Fail with High-Value Women: The Collapse of Polarity Intelligence

The question isn't "How do I get her?"
The question is: **Why does your field fail to register as reality to her nervous system?**

Most men do not fail because of looks, money, or status.
They fail because they violate the Law of Polarity. They do not understand the sacred mechanics between **pursuit, magnetization, and attachment**—and in their confusion, they short-circuit the entire magnetic sequence.

This is not a game of charm. It is a science of field dynamics.
A woman of true value does not respond to force. She responds to **coherence**—and coherence has a sequence.

## Pursue vs. Magnetize vs. Attach: Which strategy works—and when?

### 1. Magnetize First. Always.

**"Be the gravity. Let her orbit."**

You never begin with pursuit.
You begin by generating such an undeniable **field**

**of presence**, clarity, sexual command, and non-neediness that women **feel your existence without your effort**.

This is **magnetism**.

In that state:

- You don't need to "win her." You already won your own energy.

- You don't reach. You select.

- You don't initiate out of emptiness. You respond out of fullness.

**Result:**
She starts testing, playing, orbiting, checking your signal—even if she doesn't understand why. This is the moment she becomes susceptible to desire—not before.

Women don't lust after men who chase.
They lust after men whose signal they **can't ignore**.

### 2. Then Pursue—but with Power, Not Hunger

"The lion doesn't hunt with desperation. He stalks with calm inevitability."

Once magnetized, **pursuit is appropriate**—but it must **come from abundance, not scarcity**.

This means:

- You move **with choice**, not need.
- You communicate **desire**, not attachment.
- You offer **invitations**, not persuasion.

She must feel:

"This man is coming toward me—but if I falter, he'll keep walking like a king."

That's pursuit from power. That's sexy.
She opens **because she knows your pursuit is not a collapse—it's a directive.**

### 3. Do Not Try to Attach—She Must Bond First

Attachment is not your job.
**Bonding is her domain.** Women bond through:

- Emotional safety
- Orgasmic vulnerability
- Depth of presence
- Consistency of signal

- Feeling chosen but not owned

Your job is not to "get attached."
Your job is to hold such a **clean, grounded, emotionally stable field**, that she begins attaching **without you trying**.

If you attach first, she questions your status.
If she attaches first, she confirms your dominance.

This is not cruelty—it is **polarity truth**.

## Formula:

| Phase | What You Do | Why It Works |
|---|---|---|
| Magnetize | Radiate presence, clarity, depth, command | She *feels you* without you chasing |
| Pursue with Precision | Invite, lead, direct—but never cling | She opens because you're **not afraid of desire**, but not consumed by it |
| Let Her Attach First | Stay sovereign as she opens | She bonds *because* you're not trying to—your power creates trust |

## The Non-Negotiables for a High-Value Woman (Male Edition)

When a **high-value woman** is looking at men—**not a wounded girl, not a validation addict, not a fantasy chaser—but a fully formed feminine force**—she is scanning the room on multiple invisible channels. She's not looking at your money or your muscles first. She's reading **energetic integrity**, **psychological maturity**, and **sexual command—in under 10 seconds**.

Below are the **non-negotiables**—the **unspoken checklist** every high-level woman is running, even if she can't articulate it. If you fail these, she may be polite—but she will never truly open to you.

### 1. Energetic Sovereignty

"Do you own your space—or are you leaking all over the room?"

A high-value woman will not yield to a man who:

- Seeks approval with his eyes
- Fidgets, over-talks, or fills silence

- Chases attention, jokes, or social dominance

She wants a man who walks in and **doesn't need to prove presence**—because his presence already has weight.

**Translation:**
She checks your nervous system before your resume.

## 2. Clarity of Direction

"Do you know who you are and where you're going?"

She doesn't need you to be a billionaire—but she needs to feel that you:

- **Move with inner command**
- Are **not confused about your mission**
- Do not outsource your decisions or identity

If you ask her, "What should we do?" more than once—she's already off you.

**Translation:**
She's not trying to lead you. She wants to follow a man who leads himself.

### 3. Emotional Structure

"Can you hold my chaos without collapsing?"

Beautiful, high-value women come with deep emotional oceans.
She will cry. She will test. She will swirl.
If you:

- Get reactive

- Try to fix her

- Judge her for being "too much"
  Then she knows **you can't handle her fullness**.

**Translation:**
If you don't have a structure, she won't trust you with her storms—or her orgasms.

### 4. Sexual Integrity and Command

"Do you want me—or do you need me to complete you?"

She can smell sexual insecurity from across the room.

If your lust:

- Leaks without direction
- Is full of hidden shame
- Comes from a need to conquer or be validated

She will **shut down or dominate you**. Period.

What she needs:

- A man who owns his desire **without apology**
- Who can hold her gaze with raw wanting—but not need
- Who can evoke turn-on without chasing it

**Translation:**
She wants to feel desired—but not required for your identity.

## 5. Discernment

"Do you value yourself enough to say no to me?"

The most beautiful women are used to men bending, apologizing, worshipping, or betraying their own truth for access.

But if you:

- Tell her "No, that doesn't work for me."
- Refuse to reward manipulative behavior
- Maintain boundaries even when her body is offered

She **starts respecting you more than anyone else in her orbit.**

**Translation:**
If she can control you, she can't trust you.

## 6. Presence Without Performance

"Can you sit in silence with me—or are you just trying to win?"

She doesn't want your jokes, flexes, status drops, or philosophical monologues.

She wants to feel:

- You're still there when the mask drops
- You're comfortable in unstructured space
- You see her, not just what she gives you

**Translation:**
Stillness is seduction. Depth is dominance.

## 7. Spiritual Alignment (Even If Not Religious)

"Are you connected to something deeper—or just playing this life game blindly?"

A high-value woman doesn't need you to go to church or chant mantras.
But she will not stay with a man who:

- Has no inner compass
- Lives for ego, power, or addiction
- Can't articulate his relationship to the divine, to death, or to meaning

**Translation:**
She wants to feel your **soul is online**—because she plans to bare hers.

## Summary:

| Non-Negotiable | What She's Checking | Her Internal Reaction |
|---|---|---|
| Energetic Sovereignty | Nervous system control | "Safe. Strong. Present." |
| Direction | Purpose + decisiveness | "I can trust his lead." |
| Emotional Structure | Reaction vs containment | "I can be all of me with him." |
| Sexual Integrity | Clean desire | "I want to surrender." |
| Discernment | Boundaries + standards | "I respect him." |
| Presence | Depth vs performance | "He sees me." |
| Spiritual Core | Soul anchored | "This is a king." |

# Chapter 6

# The "Monetized Beauty" Woman – Psychological and Energetic Blueprint

## PART I:

This is the **archetype of the transactional feminine**—a woman who weaponizes beauty to extract material, emotional, or social currency. Her entire system is built around **external validation**, **hypergamy**, and **control via male desire**.

**Psychological Traits**

- **Beauty as Power**: She has learned that her looks trigger immediate male response. This gives her an inflated sense of control—but little self-knowledge.

- **Attachment to Lifestyle, Not Love**: Her worth is fused with access to status symbols—cars, cash, gifts, luxury environments. She does not seek intimacy; she seeks access.

- **Hyper-Promiscuity with Emotional Detachment**: She is not emotionally connected to her sexual activity. Sex is negotiation, strategy, or compliance for gain—not sacred, not relational.

- **Masculine Mimicry**: In her hunger for control and dominance, she often mimics masculine energy—assertive, transactional, and emotionally blunted.

- **Disloyalty by Design**: She is loyal only to whoever offers the most at the moment. She has **no inner principle of relational honor**—only performance-based allegiance.

This is not "evil"—it's **survival-mode femininity** in a commodified world.

## Energetic Structure (Sephirothic Diagnostic)

| Sephirah | Distortion |
|---|---|
| Netzach | Hyper-activated sensual desire, turned into seduction-for-profit |
| Yesod | Crystallized false identity built on external appearance |
| Tiphereth | Dormant causal Self; no real individuality developed |
| Malkuth | Over-anchored in materialism and embodiment, with no upward connection |
| Hod | Verbal manipulation or over-calculation to maximize gain |
| Binah | Blocked—no moral or structural compass governs behavior |

# The High-Value Man's Posture Around Monetized Beauty Women

# PART II

A **true high-value man** is not **seduced**, **angered**, or **impressed** by these women. He sees them clearly, interacts without flinching, and **never gives away his power**. Here's how:

### 1. Recognize the Game Without Judging the Player

"She's not evil. She's operating on survival software. I simply don't feed it."

High-value men don't moralize, and they don't become rescuers. They observe, assess, and hold energetic clarity.

- Don't try to save her.
- Don't try to fix her.
- Don't try to shame her.

You simply **don't offer your life force** to a system that converts it into rent payments and Instagram clout.

## 2. Control the Frame – Never Let Her Control the Narrative

She will test:

- "Can I extract from you?"
- "Can I make you compete?"
- "Can I get emotional leverage?"

You must project:

- "I don't respond to manipulation."
- "You can't emotionally bait me."
- "I value sovereignty more than sex."

**Frame dominance is everything.** She is used to setting the rules. When you **walk outside the script**, she loses control—and either escalates or leaves.

## 3. Never Validate the Beauty She's Weaponizing

"You're beautiful. But that's the least interesting thing about you."

This destroys her entire leverage strategy.

If you:

- Compliment her looks
- Fawn over her body
- Get excited by her validation
You've lost.

Instead:

- Notice, but don't reward
- Be curious, not captivated
- Focus on what she doesn't show, not what she flaunts

Women who sell sex for currency crave men they can't buy or seduce.
That's your edge.

## 4. Operate From Complete Non-Neediness

The moment she senses:

- You're trying to impress
- You're hoping for access
- You're emotionally invested in outcome

She categorizes you as a **resource**, not a man.

The high-value man is different:

"If we connect, we connect. If not, I lose nothing. I don't seek access to you—you seek alignment with me."

That energy causes her to stutter—because it's **not for sale**.

## 5. Mirror Her Subtle Desperation Without Insulting Her

Most high-level transactional women are deeply insecure.
Their survival strategy is seductive—but the **soul behind it is hollow**.

You can hold a mirror by saying:

"You're used to men chasing you.
But I wonder who you'd be if no one rewarded the image."

Or:

"You've monetized your beauty perfectly. But what part of you isn't for sale?"

If you say this **without judgment or ego**, she'll remember it for life.

## Summary: High-Value Man's Code Around Monetized Women

| Principle | Action |
|---|---|
| **See clearly** | Understand her strategy without judgment |
| **Hold center** | Never react, chase, or flatter |
| **Neutralize her power** | Don't validate her beauty or performance |
| **Speak truth without flinching** | Say what no one else has the spine to say |
| **Stay untouchable** | Never let your identity hinge on her response |
| **Withdraw attention at will** | She must feel that *you could disappear without emotion* |

**If she cannot extract from you, and she cannot control you, and she cannot seduce you—she either collapses or transforms.**

Either way, you stay **clean**, **clear**, and **undiminished**.

Chapter 6

# How to Test if She's Redeemable

(Can this monetized-beauty woman awaken and transform?)

Not all transactional women are beyond reclamation. Some are **trapped souls in a profit costume**, acting out survival code due to childhood wounding, culture, or early success in manipulation. But how do you know?

Here's the gold-standard test:

## Redeemable Signs (Green Lights)

| Signal | Why It Matters |
|---|---|
| Breaks character around your presence | If her sexual performance *drops* around you and she gets quieter, realer, more uncertain—that's the soul cracking through |
| Responds to depth without deflecting | If you offer real presence and she doesn't mock or dodge it—that's a sign she *remembers herself* |
| Asks questions about purpose, identity, or values | This shows a hidden yearning for meaning—not just survival or control |
| Sits in silence without performing | If she can endure stillness, even awkwardly, it means you're reaching past her mask |

## Non-Redeemable Signs (Red Lights)

| Signal | What It Means |
|---|---|
| Constantly sexualizes herself around you even when uninvited | Her nervous system is hard-wired to bait, not bond |
| Mocks virtue, purpose, or spiritual talk | Her ego is defending its throne—she will poison your values if allowed close |
| Can't tolerate not being the center of male attention | This is addiction, not lifestyle—she can't choose monogamy because attention is her drug |
| Uses vulnerability only to manipulate | If she "opens up" only when she's losing power, this is a trap door tactic—not transformation |

## The Final Test (The Mirror of Sovereignty)

Say something like:

"I see you. But I don't chase illusions.
You're beautiful—but I'm watching to see if there's anything behind it you haven't sold."

**Then withdraw.**
No contact. No validation. No anger.

If she returns—not with seduction, but with silence, questions, or truth—she might be redeemable.
If she ghosts or gets hostile—you just saved yourself years.

## How to Extract Value Without Being Drained

Let's say you're around these women socially, professionally, or even sexually—but don't want to give away your **power, energy, or money**.

You can still extract **signal, learning, leverage**, and even pleasure—but without falling into their trap.

### 1. Never Pay to Play—But Let Them Reveal the Game

Don't buy the fantasy. But study how it works.

Use them as a **mirror for where men lose sovereignty.** Ask:

- "What's the bait?"

- "Where do men collapse?"

- "What does she respond to versus what she ignores?"

This is **power training**—watching manipulation without submitting to it.

### 2. Control the Frame Always

- You don't buy dinner—you invite to your table.

- You don't ask for attention—you see who shows up without bait.

- You don't respond to sex games—you escalate or retreat based on your standards, not hers.

You are the sun. She orbits, or she fades.

### 3. Use Her as a Catalyst—Not a Crutch

Many beautiful, broken women trigger something primal. Use it.

Ask:

- "Why did this energy activate me?"

- "What illusion did I project onto her?"

- "What part of me still wants to be needed, praised, or chosen?"

**Extract the upgrade. Don't repeat the loop.**

## How to Train Other Men to Walk Away

High-value men must become protectors of **energetic clarity**—not just for themselves, but for other men who are still caught in the trap.

Here's how to build that culture:

### 1. Show the Difference Between Beauty and Value

"She looks like heaven—but carries no soul."

Teach men how to decode:

- **False femininity** (beauty weaponized for gain)
- **True femininity** (warmth, radiance, receptivity, soul)

**Rule of thumb**:

If her power is purely visual, her cost will be spiritual.

## 2. Create Emotional Detachment Training

Let young men:

- Interact with these women without praise
- Withhold validation
- Feel the emptiness behind the interaction

Let them **feel the illusion collapse** through direct, conscious exposure—not abstinence.

## 3. Use Brotherhood as Polarity Reset

Build small groups where men:

- Call each other out for simping, chasing, or performing
- Practice stillness around beauty
- Reflect honestly on where they collapsed or gave power away

Brotherhood is the gym for polarity calibration.

**4. Give Them This Law:**

**You're not a man because you can get her.
You're a man because you can walk away from her.**

Until a man can walk away from the most physically beautiful woman in the room without regret, **he is still her slave.**

**These women only control men who are already fragmented.**
The high-value man is not tempted—because he is already full.

He doesn't need her beauty.
He doesn't fear her power.
And when he speaks to her soul instead of her image—**he either liberates her or exposes her.**

Both are victories.

# Chapter 7

# The Elite Field Manual

Below is a complete, field-ready, elite-level system to teach young men how to:
1. **Recognize women prone to affairs or one-night stands**

2. **Capitalize if desired (ethically)**

3. **Protect themselves if they don't want to be used or cheated on**

4. **Understand the exact type of man women target for short-term sex or secret affairs**


**PART I: WOMEN PRONE TO AFFAIRS / ONE-NIGHT STANDS**

**Personality, Behavior, and Signal Patterns**

These women are not "bad"—but they are **strategically opportunistic** in love and sex. Most fall into one of three categories:

## Type A: The Hyper-Validation Seeker

She uses sex to **prove her desirability**, especially when emotionally unfulfilled.

**Tells and Traits:**

- Constant social media presence (especially seductive photos)

- Subtle sexual energy even in normal conversations

- Flirty with everyone, not just you

- Often mentions how men hit on her, how she gets attention, or how exes "regret losing her"

- Over-complains about her current man's lack of appreciation

These women cheat not out of lust—but to feel wanted again.
**Key Phrase:** "He just doesn't see me anymore."

## Type B: The Erotic Adventurer (Impulse Junkie)

She's thrill-seeking, ruled by desire and novelty.

**Tells and Traits:**

- Lots of spontaneous tattoos, piercings, or travel stories
- Quick to escalate touch, innuendo, or drinking
- Feels emotionally shallow but sexually alive
- Uses phrases like: "Life is short," "No regrets," or "I follow energy"

These women are down for one-night stands, often guilt-free.
**Key Phrase:** "I do what feels right in the moment."

## Type C: The Emotional Affair Hunter (Shadow Connector)

These are women in relationships or marriages who form **deep emotional bonds with other men**—then rationalize crossing lines.

**Tells and Traits:**

- Vents about her partner in a soft, almost intimate way
- Says "you understand me better than anyone" early
- Seeks long talks, secrets, late-night texting, subtle emotional dependency
- Will say things like: "I've never felt this safe before" or "You just get me"

This is the most dangerous type—because the man believes "it's just emotional." Then sex happens. **Key Phrase:** "I'm not sure what this is, but it feels real."

## PART II: HOW TO CAPITALIZE — IF YOU CHOOSE TO

If a man **consciously chooses** to engage with this type of woman (no shame, just strategy), he must understand **what she is seeking** and **how to become it temporarily**, without entanglement.

Chapter 7

# Attributes of the Man She'll Choose for Affairs or One-Night Stands

| Trait | Why She Chooses It |
|---|---|
| Emotionally Tethered But Unattached | He can offer intimacy or arousal without asking for a relationship |
| Physically Confident | She needs the **animal signal**: strong frame, controlled aggression, eye contact |
| Unavailable or Unapologetically Sovereign | Ironically, being slightly *hard to access* makes her pursue *you* as the escape |
| Smooth Non-Reactivity | She feels safe being messy, flirty, or bold because you won't judge or overreact |
| Dominant but Safe | She wants to surrender without feeling stupid or unsafe |

## Translation:

She doesn't want a boyfriend—she wants **a mirror of her repressed longing**.
The more you feel like an undeniable experience, the more likely she is to cross the line.

## Warning: If You Choose This Path

- **Set the frame early**: "I'm not looking for commitment."

- **No emotional messaging**: Stay off her phone late at night.

- **Never chase**: The minute you chase, she loses interest.

- **Withdraw cleanly**: No ghosting—just clarity. "That was real, but not for forever."

## PART III: HOW TO PROTECT YOURSELF — If You're NOT Trying to Be That Guy

If you're a man who doesn't want to:

- Be cheated with

- Get used as a sexual object

- Or fall for a woman who's likely to betray

Then these are the **field-level defense protocols**:

### 1. Watch How She Talks About Her Past Men

If every ex is a villain—she has no self-awareness. If she was the cheater before—**she still is**. No one "grows out" of it without inner healing.

## 2. Test Her for Loyalty Before It's Needed

See how she acts when you're busy, emotionally unavailable, or out of contact.

- If she complains, flirts elsewhere, or gets passive-aggressive—she needs constant attention. That's a risk.

- A woman who stays emotionally secure when you're distant is far more trustworthy.

## 3. Audit Her Social Media

Her Instagram is her real journal.

- High volume of thirst traps = external validation loop

- DM responses from male "fans" = constant attention reinforcement

- If she posts more of herself than her life, she's not present—she's performing

## 4. Don't Sleep with Her Too Fast

If you hold your frame and delay sex:

- She either respects it and leans in (green flag)
- Or she gets annoyed and ghosts (red flag = she wanted fast dopamine)

# PART IV: TEACHING YOUNG MEN – IDENTIFICATION CHART

| Woman Type | Signal | What To Do |
| --- | --- | --- |
| Validation-Seeker | Always needs praise, "Do you still think I'm pretty?" | Set boundaries, test consistency |
| Erotic Adventurer | Says "I just go with the flow," touches fast | Enjoy *only if you can detach* |
| Emotional Affair Type | Deep convos too soon, "You get me" energy | Guard your heart, or get pulled into shadow bonding |
| Real One | Respectful, sensual but not performative, filters men | Proceed slowly, build with honor |

Chapter 7

## CLOSING: THE LAW OF MASCULINE CLARITY

A man who knows what he wants will never be misused by a woman who doesn't.

You don't need to control women—you need to **read energy, enforce standards, and hold frame**.
Women will always reveal who they are.
It's up to the man to decide whether to:

- **Engage for experience**

- **Invite transformation**

- Or **walk away without reaction**

# Chapter 8

## THE HIGH-VALUE MAN'S FIELD CODE

Below is your **Field Code Card**—a **pocket-sized mental framework** for entering any space where high-beauty, monetized, or manipulative feminine energy may appear. Whether it's a club, VIP event, dinner party, or social scene—this card will keep your polarity clean, your power intact, and your standards untouchable.

**Carry this. Memorize this. Live this.**

### 1. I Am the Prize, Not the Seeker.

I do not orbit beauty.
Beauty orbits me.
My presence is the access point—not my desire.

**Metaphysical Decoding of Field Code 1**

This is not arrogance. It is the restoration of divine order. Inverting the chase dynamic is not about pride—it is about polarity. The masculine is the fixed axis; the feminine is the field of motion. When a man forgets this, he begins to revolve around image, body, and fantasy, losing his central position in the cosmic wheel.

To say "I am the prize" is not to make a claim of superiority—it is to reclaim the **central seat of law**.

It is to recognize that the masculine carries the structure, the standard, and the seed of meaning. The seeker posture is inverted masculine. It is the energetic signature of a man who has externalized his authority and now moves as a satellite to female validation, beauty, or chaos.

When you remember that **your presence is the access point**, you move like a sovereign. You are not trying to gain admission into her world—you are the world she enters when she is ready to rise. You do not chase; you radiate. You do not orbit; you magnetize. This is not passive, nor is it performative. It is a **spinal knowing**. A metaphysical stillness that makes all motion orbit around it.

To live this first code is to **collapse the illusion of sexual scarcity**, to **disidentify from the predator-prey economy**, and to **re-anchor your worth in soul signal, not social hierarchy**. You do not get chosen. You emanate. And in that emanation, the feminine is given the choice to mirror you or be repelled by you—but you are never moved.

This is not strategy. It is **ontological remembrance**. You do not need to impress what you already embody.

## 2. I Validate Nothing That Is Weaponized.

If it's flaunted, I don't chase it.
If it's bait, I let it rot.
I see behind the image—and I stay silent.

**Metaphysical Decoding of Field Code 2:**

Validation is energy. Attention is currency. When either is granted to an image that is designed to manipulate, the man collapses into a false contract: one where he plays the buyer, and the feminine plays the seller of worth.

To validate the flaunted, the baited, or the weaponized is to **bend the knee to illusion**. It is to become a consumer of symbolic power, rather than a generator of true essence. Weaponized beauty is not a feminine sin—it is a masculine failure. A failure to discern signal from spell. A failure to preserve the authority of one's gaze. A failure to **anchor one's crown in structure rather than sensuality**.

When a man chases what is flaunted, he devalues his inner court. He becomes a responder to external displays. He moves from King to pawn in a rigged game of desirability. But when he **lets the bait rot**, when he refuses to feed illusions with even a drop of attention, he collapses the energetic economy that seeks to feed on his instability.

This is not about suppressing attraction—it's about **discerning alchemy from advertisement**.

Weaponized femininity always comes with an energetic invoice. It demands a payment of frame—or one's internal gravitational structure that governs how perception, attention, and decisions are anchored—as well as clarity, and sometimes even mission. The man who does not see this becomes a **subscriber to seduction**, a node in someone else's mirror loop.

The man who sees through it but says nothing—he is not passive, he is dominant. Silence is not weakness here. It is **polaric compression**. It is the refusal to play. It is the commandment that says: I will not spend myself on what is inflated, inverted, or insecurely projected.

This code trains you to **listen to structure, not seduction**. It teaches you to smell the frequency of unintegrated feminine power—and to keep your throne sealed unless it is honored through depth, not display. True feminine radiance does not bait—it invites. It does not perform—it blesses. And if it must beg, flash, or provoke, it is not ready to enter your field.

Your gaze is sacred. Do not spend it where chaos is dressed as confidence.

### 3. I Speak Sparingly, But with Weight.

I never perform. I never over-explain.
My words are calibrated.
I enter the room as a **signal**, not a question.

### Metaphysical Decoding of Field Code 3

Words are not tools of approval. They are structures of command. When a man speaks from King frequency, his speech is not a performance—it is a signal. It calibrates the space. It tells the feminine, the field, and the forces: This is where I stand. This is what I allow. This is what ends here.

In a world of performative validation and reactive expression, the high-value man becomes rare by his **verbal restraint**. He understands that the more he speaks to gain approval, the more he leaks his axis. The more he over-explains, the more he abdicates the throne. Every unnecessary word becomes a **payment of power**—a signal that his inner court is not yet sealed.

To speak sparingly is not silence born of fear—it is **speech forged by structure**. Each word is passed through multiple internal filters: Is it necessary? Is it directional? Is it clean of need? Is it coded with purpose? If not, it is discarded. The man becomes a sovereign editor of his own vibration.

This is more than communication—it is **field regulation**. In the presence of unintegrated feminine energy, verbal overcompensation is often an unconscious strategy to please, soften, or prove worth. But the man who has burned his mimicry and fused his core knows: **the room is already calibrated when he enters**. There is no need to compensate. His eye contact says what his words don't. His silence bends timelines. His frequency transmits laws long before his mouth opens.

This level of masculine presence creates psychic contrast. The feminine may first experience it as tension. But in that tension is the safety she has never known—the safety of a man who is not for sale, not for flattery, and not for fantasy. His words don't seek access—they **guard access**. And when he speaks, he speaks **as a gatekeeper**, not a guest.

The King's voice is not loud. It is **anchored**. Not performative—**precise**. It is not for show—it is for transmission. One sentence from this kind of man can shift the emotional chemistry of a space. Because it's not just the words—it's the clarity of the source they come from.

Train your words until they become weapons of order. Not entertainment. Not seduction. Not fear-masking fluff.

Speak less. Say more.

## 4. My Attention Is the Currency—She Can't Afford Me.

I give presence only to the woman who earns it through radiance, depth, and humility.
Not beauty. Not performance. Not thirst.

**Metaphysical Decoding of Field Code 4**

Attention is not neutral. It is not casual. It is not free.

Your gaze, your listening, your focused presence—these are **primary energetic currencies** that reveal where your sovereignty is invested. A man who does not regulate his attention has no inner treasury. He leaks value before value is earned. He pays full price for projections. He feeds illusions with full eye contact. And he bankrupts his masculine radiance chasing surface performance.

The true high-value man knows this: **his attention is sacred**. Not because it is rare, but because it is filtered. He does not offer presence to every woman who performs femininity. He does not gift focus to those who manipulate image while abandoning substance. He does not reward surface with soul.

Instead, he becomes **the gatekeeper of his awareness**. He measures not beauty—but **depth**. Not display—but **devotion**. Not allure—but **alignment**. His attention is earned by feminine resonance—not requested by feminine performance.

This level of discernment activates a higher polarity in the field. The woman who is used to being chased will either **collapse or awaken**. Collapse if her identity is built on validation. Awaken if her essence is waiting to be seen without distortion. In either case, your standard becomes **the test**. And your silence becomes **the mirror**.

To hold this frequency, a man must be willing to **withhold the gaze**. To protect his awareness from fragmented seduction. To let radiance pass unengaged when it is not backed by reverence. This does not mean shaming beauty—but **dethroning it**. No longer worshiping the aesthetic above the authentic.

When a man moves through the world with this lens, his presence becomes a **consecrated space**. A space the feminine must rise to meet—not fall into by default. This is not arrogance—it is architecture. He is not punishing her for performance—he is **refusing to fund it**.

He knows the truth: women are not awakened by being pursued. They are awakened by being filtered. **By a man whose standard calls her soul forward**. Not her mask. Not her mimicry. Not her social value—but her essence.

And if that essence is not there, he walks.

No negotiation. No collapse. No apology.

Because she cannot afford the price of a man whose value is not printed in lust, likes, or longing—but in **discipline, structure, and self-honoring stillness**.

His attention is the currency. And the kingdom it funds is sacred.

## 5. I Know the Difference Between Lust and Leadership.

I feel desire without collapsing into it.
I do not chase sex.
I offer an invitation—and I walk away clean if it's declined.

### Metaphysical Decoding of Field Code 5

Lust is impulse.
Leadership is structure.
One collapses. The other constructs.

In a world where feminine performance is often engineered to provoke reaction, the uninitiated man mistakes his arousal for authority. He feels a surge of desire and believes it is a signal to pursue. But this reaction is not power—it is programming.

**Lust is externalized hunger**. It pulls the masculine off his axis and into the orbit of the feminine image. It makes him responsive rather than sovereign. It tricks him into believing that chasing beauty makes him bold, when in fact—it makes him disposable. For what he pursues without purpose, he cannot contain with power.

Leadership, by contrast, is not anti-desire. It is **regulated desire**. It sees beauty, feels the pull—but stands rooted in direction. The high-value man does not shut down lust. He **filters it** through law. He converts it into clarity, not collapse.

He understands that desire must pass a **threshold of worthiness** before it is given an offering. And even then, it is not gifted out of thirst, but out of choice. It is not spilled for validation, but structured for initiation. It is not used to impress—but to test.

When a man confuses lust with leadership, he chases sex thinking it proves power. But in truth, **every time he collapses into lust without structure, he forfeits the throne of his nervous system**. He trains his biology to respond to seduction rather than spirit. He builds no kingdom—only conquests. He becomes the hunted, not the holder.

True masculine leadership is the ability to feel everything—and collapse into nothing.
To see the lips, hips, scent, and spell—and remain architected.
To offer the invitation from a grounded place—and to walk away clean when it is not met.

This is not coldness. It is **command**.
Not repression. But **refinement**.

It is the ability to hold a sacred frequency that calls the feminine into reverence—not into performance. Because the man who leads with structure, not seduction, becomes the altar—not the audience. The oracle—not the observer.

He does not lose his power in the pursuit.
He expands it through discernment.

And that discernment is what separates the **initiated king** from the **lust-trapped boy**.

## 6. I Read the Energy, Not the Body.

I look past the hips, lips, legs, and lashes.
I listen to her *structure.
If I sense disorder, mimicry, or manipulation—I shut the portal.

### Metaphysical Decoding of Field Code 6

The body is the bait.
The energy is the architecture.

Uninitiated men are trained by the outer world to respond to the visible—skin, curves, lashes, lips. They do not see the structure behind the surface. They do not sense the psychic frame that holds the beauty in place—or distorts it. They are ruled by **image**, not **essence**. This is the blindness of the lust-programmed masculine.

But the High-Value Man reads differently.

He reads the ***charge behind the smile**.
He decodes the **disorder behind the flirtation**.
He sees whether beauty is a transmission—or a trap.

This is not paranoia. It is **pattern recognition** rooted in metaphysical clarity. Feminine beauty can be sacred invitation—or spiritual mimicry. And often, the more exaggerated the external, the more chaotic the internal.

The man who lacks this lens will fall for the seductress masked as a mystic.
He will believe the embodied magnetism of a wounded woman is "divine feminine," when it is actually unintegrated force looking to devour a host.
He will confuse sexual availability for soul openness—and pay the price in psychic leakage, distorted polarity, and energetic depletion.

But the initiated man is not hypnotized by hips.
He is not spellbound by lashes.
He listens to **tone**, not tone of voice.
He watches **alignment**, not aesthetics.
He senses **chaos** in polished performances—and he withdraws before being entangled.

He knows when the beauty is a signal of embodiment...
...and when it is a costume stitched over collapse.

This Field Code protects the man's most sacred resource: **his presence**. Because presence is not just attention—it is an **energy technology**. And if he grants that presence to a body with no spiritual container, he will bleed out his power with every glance, reply, or reaction.

So he *filters with frequency, not fantasy.
He measures the soul, not the symmetry.
And when his gut speaks—he listens.

This is how he protects the kingdom.
This is how he honors the throne.
This is how he **becomes the filter**, instead of being filtered by lust.

He does not try to awaken women who are entangled in illusion.
He does not try to fix the feminine when she is inverted.
He simply reads the code—and either offers a clean mirror or exits the system.

That is power.
That is discernment.
That is structure in the field.

***Footnote:** Structure - i.e., the underlying psychic architecture or energetic scaffolding that holds her being in coherence—beyond looks or performance.

Charge - the subtle emotional voltage or unresolved psychic content radiating beneath a person's expression or aura.

Filters with frequency - meaning he discerns based on vibrational resonance—what is spiritually aligned or dissonant—not based on fantasy, form, or desire

## 7. If I Can't Walk Away, I Don't Belong There.

No woman is my god.
No image is my home.
No body is worth the betrayal of my self-mastery.

**Metaphysical Decoding of Field Code 7**

This is not a line.
This is a litmus test of sovereignty.

In every domain—sexual, spiritual, social—the masculine is only magnetic when it is free. That freedom is not emotional detachment. It is structural autonomy. The ability to withdraw one's field from any environment, person, or temptation **without fragmentation** is the sign that the inner throne is intact.

A man who cannot walk away from beauty is not a king—he is a hostage.

This Field Code exposes the **false idols of the external feminine**: the woman whose image becomes a shrine, whose attention becomes a drug, whose approval becomes a leash. When the masculine is uninitiated, it confuses magnetic intensity for divine union—and surrenders not out of leadership, but from lack of self.

This is the collapse of spiritual gravity.
This is how kingdoms are lost.

## Chapter 8

To walk away is not an act of aggression.
It is the highest form of calibration.

It means:

- You recognize when her energy threatens your *structure
- You see the hidden contracts woven through seduction
- You are no longer worshiping her body at the expense of your code

Walking away does not mean abandoning the feminine. It means refusing to collapse for it. The man who collapses, clings. The man who clings, bleeds power. The man who bleeds power loses polarity—and the throne he was never ready to hold.

Initiation requires thresholds. This is one of them.

There will be women whose presence activates your childhood wounds.
Women who project god-like significance onto you.
Women whose bodies mirror your fantasies.
Women whose emotional volatility keeps you "working" for peace.

And if you stay—without sovereignty—you will be absorbed.

This Field Code breaks the contract of **worship-through-lack**. It reinstates the inner law: no external woman is God. No body is home. No face is worth betrayal of your throne.

If you cannot walk away, you have already given away the scepter.
If you refuse to walk away, you are not the chooser—you are the chosen.
And if you do walk away, the Universe confirms: **you were always the architect, never the addict**.

This is the masculine spine.
This is the divine audit of polarity.
This is the firewall that separates a man who leads from a man who longs.

He does not stay where his soul contracts.
He does not worship what tests his crown.
He does not entertain frequency inversion, no matter how exquisite the form.

If he cannot walk away, he does not belong there.

\*Footnote:

**structure:** the internal architecture of a being's coherence—composed of his principles, boundaries, energetic containment, and the continuity of his sovereign will. It is the metaphysical spine that holds his identity united rather than fragmented. When "structure" is threatened, it means his inner alignment is at risk of bending, leaking, or reorganizing itself around another's emotional field instead of remaining self-governed.

## 8. I Let My Frame Break Her Fantasy—Or Her Spell Break Itself.

If she's redeemable, my clarity will awaken her.
If she's not, my silence will dissolve her.

Either way—**I remain sovereign.**

I never chase.
I never compete.
I never collapse.
I **see.**
I **filter.**
I **lead.**
I **leave when needed.**


### Metaphysical Decoding of Field Code 8

This is not game. This is *geometry.

Every woman arrives in your field carrying a structure—visible or hidden. That structure may be a fantasy she is addicted to, or a spell she is unconsciously under. Either way, she will test your presence not to provoke weakness, but to measure what law governs your realm.

If your *frame is unformed, her fantasy wins.
If your *frame is reactive, her spell wins.
If your *frame is sovereign—everything else dissolves.

This Field Code is the masculine firewall. It means you do not adjust your gravity to accommodate her delusion. You do not dilute your signal to avoid conflict. You do not pacify her chaos hoping to be chosen. You enter as a stabilizing frequency—and if her nervous system or psyche is not calibrated to it, she will either rise or retreat.

That is the law of polarity. Not manipulation—**metaphysical filtration**.

Many women are unknowingly enslaved to archetypal wounds:

- The fantasy of the "perfect man" who gives without leading

- The fantasy of a "safe space" where she can control the dynamic

- The spell of self-protection dressed as independence

- The echo of prior abandonment disguised as intuition

She may carry these into your field like sacred truths. But they are false pillars. And if you accommodate them, you reinforce her exile. You reward her distortion. You participate in her unreality.

This Field Code denies the counterfeit.

## Chapter 8

It means:

- You do not become the man she imagines—you remain the one who is

- You do not soften your backbone to protect her illusions

- You do not chase after clarity—you reveal it by standing still

Her fantasy, if it has no root in divine structure, must break when confronted with a man who embodies one. Not through aggression. Not through arrogance. But through lawful stillness. Through the silent thunder of your frame, which says:
**"I am not here to fit your script. I am the end of scripts."**

Your field becomes a diagnostic mirror.
If she is redeemable, your presence purifies her.
If she is not, she will break contact—not because you failed, but because your code revealed the lie she depended on.

The modern man is taught to adapt to a woman's world.
The initiated man invites her into his.
He does not ask, "What is her story?"
He simply emits law—and lets her fantasy collapse or convert.

This is how the true masculine corrects feminine fragmentation.

Not by explaining himself.
Not by psychoanalyzing her wounds.
Not by fixing her chaos.
But by letting it fracture against his frame.

He walks into the room as structure.
He speaks only when alignment requires it.
He does not join the dream. He becomes the awakening.

This is not cruelty. This is divine compassion through structure.

If she is still under spell—your field will feel like violence.
If she is ready for throne—your field will feel like home.

Either way—you remain intact.
Either way—you do not chase.
Either way—you win by remaining who you are.

## The Field Code + The Vortex:

Every line in the **Field Code** is designed to preserve the vortex.

- **"I do not orbit beauty. Beauty orbits me."**
  —Preserves the **Atzelooothic signal** from being inverted by external desire.

- **"I read the energy, not the body."**
  —Refuses to let the **Yetziratic illusions** (mimicry, cosmetic signals, auric projections) scramble the signal.

- **"If I can't walk away, I don't belong there."**
  —Prevents **Assiatic collapse** into ego-bound action.

This isn't performance.
This is **polarity recursion** in action.

*Footnote:

**Frame** - is the psychic container a man holds around himself—it is the sum total of his values, boundaries, spiritual architecture, and embodied truth. It is invisible structure made visible through conduct, word, silence, and stance. It does not react—it calibrates.

**Geometry** - refers to the active relational pattern by which a being expresses inner coherence across dimensions. It is not a possession, not a technique, and not a spiritual state one "enters." It is the **metaphysical signature of internal proportion**—the exact alignment between thought, will, emotion, energy, and action.

To say a person carries divine geometry means their inner pattern reflects higher law: their choices, movements, desires, and realizations unfold with causal symmetry rather than randomness. Their being is integrated instead of scattered; their will fires in alignment instead of erratic impulse. Their life displays timing, pattern, and precision that reveal the workings of higher intelligence through them.

A being out of alignment expresses broken geometry: contradiction, emotional fragmentation, obsessive thought loops, sexual leakage, collapse under pressure, and karmic entanglements. This is not the absence of geometry—it is geometry in distortion: proportion collapsed, ratios inverted, signals incoherent.

A being aligned with higher causation expresses refined geometry: an internal ratio that mirrors the architecture of the cosmos. Their pattern becomes recursive; the microcosm reflects the macrocosm. Their presence bends behavior, perception, attraction, and destiny because their inner laws and outer movement share the same causative proportion. They do not perform order—they emanate it.

Geometry, in this system, is therefore the **exact pattern of forces a being broadcasts**—the measurable coherence by which they generate synchronicity, influence polarity, alter fields, and become detectable to the higher lattice of reality.

# Chapter 9

## BUSINESS MAGNETISM BLUEPRINT

### I. Magnetism as Market Architecture

The ultra-magnetic man doesn't just exist in the economy — he reshapes the economy around himself. He becomes a **market node**: people, money, and opportunities reroute through him as if he is infrastructure.

- Normal men "work in" a system.

- Clever men "exploit" a system.

- Magnetic men **become the system others must move through.**

This is why the most magnetic in business history create empires: they stop being "players" and become "environment." Everyone else negotiates with each other. They negotiate with him.

**Law:** True business magnetism is not being good at the game. It is becoming the board.

## II. The Law of Asymmetry

In business, everyone is trading on symmetry: time for money, product for price, skill for contract. The magnetic man bends reality because he moves asymmetrically.

- He creates **offers that cannot be compared.**

- He generates **leverage points that tilt entire industries.**

- He refuses to play in categories where parity is possible.

This makes him impossible to price-shop, replace, or negotiate down. While others are stuck in "competitive markets," his very presence defines a new category.

**Translation:** Magnetism in business is the art of making yourself incomparable.

## III. Capital as Confirmation of Essence

Money does not reward need, labor, or even genius. It rewards **the signal of inevitability.**

- Investors want to feel they already missed out if they don't align with you.

- Clients want to feel that refusing you would cost them more than paying you.

- Partners want to feel they'll look weaker without you than stronger with you.

This is not "sales." This is essence. The magnetic man's money-flows are proof of his inevitability.

**Law:** Money is not proof you worked. Money is proof you became impossible to ignore.

## IV. The Archetype of the Economic Oracle

Magnetic men in business are not just leaders or entrepreneurs. They are oracles. They read patterns others cannot see, and then embody them before anyone else is ready.

- He doesn't predict the market. He is the early tremor of the new market.

- Others call him "lucky" or "visionary." In truth, he is structurally attuned to the next order of reality.

- He bends not only profits but culture.

The secret is not foresight — it is **alignment with inevitability before it becomes visible.**

### V. Field Effects in Business

The magnetic man changes economics **by existing**.

- **In rooms:** Meetings run faster. Conflicts collapse. Timelines compress.

- **In negotiations:** The other side feels "time is running out" even when it isn't.

- **In markets:** Competitors orbit him by default, reacting to his moves before he makes them.

This is field law: business magnetism is the invisible acceleration of other people's decisions in your favor.

### VI. The Shadow of Business Magnetism

- **The Hustler Mask:** Performs dominance, attracts quick capital, collapses under scrutiny.

- **The Mimic:** Copies the styles of magnetic men, wins applause but never trust.

- **The Addict:** Treats business magnetism as power-drug, weaponizes charm, leaves scorched earth.

**Law:** False magnetism profits fast but dies young. True magnetism profits slow but rewrites the entire system.

## VII. The Seal of Business Magnetism

Business magnetism is not about charisma or grind. It is about becoming a **structural inevitability.**

- If you are optional, you will be ignored.
- If you are comparable, you will be underpriced.
- If you are replaceable, you will be replaced.
- But if you are **inevitable**, the world must pay to orbit you.

"In business, magnetism is not who they like. It is who they cannot move without."

# Chapter 10

**BROTHERHOOD MAGNETISM BLUEPRINT**

The ultra-magnetic man is not only axis for women or orbit for markets. Among men, he becomes **organizing principle.** Brotherhood either forms around him, or collapses in his absence.

## I. The Law of Male Alignment

Other men are always scanning unconsciously: "If war broke out right now, who would I stand behind?"

- They are not looking for charm.
- They are not looking for talent.
- They are looking for **structural backbone.**

This is why men follow not the loudest, not the richest, but the one who feels like **the hinge between order and chaos.**

**Law:** Brotherhood magnetism is measured by how many men instinctively brace behind you when pressure hits.

## II. The Three Archetypes of Male Magnetism

1. **The Standard** – He sets the unspoken law of what is acceptable. If he refuses weakness, no one else indulges it. If he shows endurance, others rise. His existence upgrades the room.

2. **The Filter** – He sorts men without saying a word. Weak men feel exposed and leave. Strong men feel sharpened and stay. Brotherhood magnetism doesn't gather crowds — it crystallizes elites.

3. **The Conductor** – He resolves male rivalry without collapsing hierarchy. He knows when to challenge, when to unify, and when to step back. His field organizes men into functional order.

## III. Brotherhood as Polarity Laboratory

Men train their polarity against other men before they can hold women or wealth.

- With brothers, you test limits of honesty.

- With rivals, you test strength of frame.

- With mentors, you test submission to clarity.

If a man cannot magnetize men, his magnetism with women or markets is fragile. Why? Because the masculine field is forged against other masculine fields.

**Translation:** Brotherhood is the gym of magnetism. Fail here, and you fail everywhere.

## IV. The Inversions of Brotherhood Magnetism

- **The Pretender** – Leans on status signals (money, women, possessions). Men tolerate him, but none trust him.

- **The Over-Dominator** – Intimidates instead of stabilizes. Creates obedience, but not loyalty. His brotherhood collapses the moment fear fades.

- **The Court Jester** – Wins laughs, never weight. Men invite him, but never follow him.

- **The Manipulator** – Plays groups against each other to maintain control. Short-term influence, long-term exile.

**Law:** If men only laugh at you, obey you, or use you — you have influence, not magnetism.

## V. The Stress Test of Brotherhood

Brotherhood magnetism is proven in three crucibles:

1. **Conflict** – Do men hide behind you or scatter when threatened?

2. **Competition** – Do rivals sharpen into allies or fracture into enemies?

3. **Absence** – When you leave the room, does order collapse or remain?

If your presence is necessary for cohesion, you are the axis. If not, you were decoration.

## VI. Brotherhood Magnetism in Practice

- In small groups: He sets tone without speech. Meetings follow his rhythm, debates collapse when he cuts in, laughter shifts when he turns serious.

- In large networks: His reputation moves faster than his presence. Men adjust before he arrives.

- In crisis: He does not flinch. His stability pulls other men into alignment faster than orders could.

This is why true magnetic men rarely speak much in brotherhoods. Their weight is coded in silence.

### VII. The Seal of Brotherhood Magnetism

Brotherhood magnetism is not about being liked, feared, or admired. It is about being the man other men unconsciously calculate around.

- Women open when they feel safe.
- Markets flow when they feel stable.
- But men organize when they feel **inevitable.**

"In brotherhood, magnetism is not dominance. It is inevitability. You are not louder than other men. You are the man they cannot move without."

# Chapter 11

# The Trinity of Magnetism: Sex, Money, Power

A magnetic man does not chase women, wealth, or influence. He stabilizes his axis, and reality reorders itself around him. What appears to others as charm, fortune, or leadership is none of these—it is the law of polarity manifesting through three currencies: sex, money, and power.

**Sex: The Body's Confession of Polarity**
The feminine body is the first instrument to register a man's field. Before thought, before choice, her pulse accelerates or softens, her gaze lingers or averts, her laughter escapes without permission. These are not preferences but involuntary recognitions: the field has spoken. Lust is not romance. It is not persuasion. It is the biological confession: "I have met a force I cannot organize. I must yield or flee."

**Money: The Market's Confession of Sovereignty**
Money does not obey hustling or need. It obeys sovereignty. It flows toward men whose presence

signals: "I cannot be bought. I cannot be rushed. I cannot be moved from my axis." The market, like the feminine, is always scanning—not for brilliance or charm, but for anchors. A man who refuses collapse becomes the safe container for circulation, and wealth confirms what is already true: his sovereignty is intact.

## Power: The Collective's Confession of Inevitability

Power is the heaviest currency. It is not seized by force; it is recognized by the collective nervous system. Men look at a field and unconsciously ask: "Who can resolve our chaos without collapsing?" The magnetic man does not declare authority; his presence organizes resistance and loyalty alike. Even enemies orbit him, for their opposition still confirms his centrality. True power is clarity so immovable that others doubt themselves before they doubt him.

## The Shadow of Magnetism

Every current carries poison if sovereignty is lost.

Sex becomes addiction when pursued as identity.

Money becomes enslavement when mistaken for validation.

Power becomes tyranny when consumed as ownership.

The moment a man collapses into hunger—

whether for bodies, gold, or obedience—he reverts from axis to beggar. The orbit dissolves, and the very forces that once adored him conspire to unseat him.

**The Seal of Sovereignty**
The ultra-magnetic man does not measure himself by women taken, money gained, or men obeying. He measures himself by the stability of his axis. Sex confirms his polarity. Money confirms his sovereignty. Power confirms his inevitability. But only sovereignty confirms his mastery. Without it, magnetism decays into seduction and collapse. With it, magnetism becomes law.

**Sex: The Erotic Confirmation of Polarity**

Sex is not a performance, not an achievement, not an external conquest. It is the **body's submission to a field**. The feminine body reads the masculine nervous system faster than the mind ever could. Long before she speaks or chooses, her breath, her pulse, her posture betray what she has already recognized: whether she is in the presence of gravity or of hunger.

A woman's lust does not emerge from rational preference—it is the collapse of vigilance before a force she cannot reorganize. Her mind may resist, her ego may argue, but her body responds to one signal only: **is this man a still axis, or another unstable satellite?**

## 1. The Nervous System as Gatekeeper

Every woman carries in her body the memory of disappointment: men who chased, men who begged, men who flattered, men who promised strength but flinched under pressure. This accumulation becomes hyper-vigilance—the constant scanning for weakness behind the mask.

The magnetic man disarms this scanning not with words, but with the **tone of his nervous system**. His steadiness under her storm—whether it is flirtation, rejection, or emotional chaos—signals: "You may release your guard. I will not collapse."

This is why women report feeling lust not when a man says the "right" line, but when he looks at her and does not break eye contact, when he moves slowly in a room while others rush, when his voice carries weight without strain. These micro-signals tell her ancient body: "You are already claimed. Not by force, but by inevitability."

## 2. Lust as the Paradox of Safety and Danger

The deepest arousal arises in paradox: a woman must feel **safe enough to open, yet threatened enough to feel taken.**

- If she feels only safety, desire flattens. He is a brother, a friend, a caretaker.

- If she feels only threat, defenses rise. He is a predator, an invader.

- But if she feels the paradox—a safe container that radiates unapologetic want— her body floods with lust.

This paradox is the essence of polarity. He communicates without speaking:

- "You are safe in my presence." (safety)

- "But I will not hide that I want to consume you." (danger)

Her body reads this as irresistible. It is not strategy—it is alignment.

### 3. Erotic Gravity vs. Erotic Need

The difference between gravity and need is the difference between kings and beggars.

- **Need** leaks through gaze that asks permission, touch that seeks reassurance, speech that over-explains. She feels she must manage him, and her body closes.

- **Gravity** is the presence that expects nothing, yet denies nothing. His eyes do not chase, but they do not hide. His silence does not beg, but it does not apologize. His touch is not hurried, but neither is it hesitant. Erotic gravity pulls her forward without words. Her breath changes. Her posture tilts toward him. The lust she feels is not "attraction to a man"—it is the surrender of a system meeting its opposite pole.

### 4. The Biology of Surrender

Science confirms what archetypes have always known: lust is not random. It is the chemical recognition of polarity.

- **Testosterone signals** (deep voice, broad stance, controlled aggression) increase female dopamine and norepinephrine—arousal, craving, tension.

- **Oxytocin triggers** (steady gaze, consistent touch, unbroken presence) release safety hormones—trust, bonding, openness.

- **Pheromonal chemistry**—the scent of confidence without cortisol stress—operates below conscious awareness.

The cocktail is precise: high testosterone without recklessness, high oxytocin without softness. The feminine body translates this as: "He could dominate me, but chooses to contain me. Therefore I can yield."


## 5. The Archetypal Lock

Behind the biology is archetype. The feminine is chaos, flow, emotion, beauty. The masculine is order, stillness, direction, sovereignty.

When these meet in clean polarity, the archetypal memory awakens: woman as ocean, man as shore. The waves crash not to destroy, but to be held. Her lust is not mere biology—it is mythic recognition: "I have found the one strong enough to receive me."

This is why lust feels holy when polarity is intact. It is not just sex; it is **the cosmos re-enacting its own creation drama**.

### 6. The Shadow of Erotic Magnetism

Magnetic men must beware: the erotic field attracts endlessly. Without discernment, sex becomes an addiction that bleeds sovereignty. Women will throw themselves at the field, not because they love him, but because they crave the relief of submission.

The danger is believing sex is proof of worth. In truth, sex is proof only of polarity. A man who confuses conquest with kingship loses both. The high-value man remembers: sex is confirmation, not identity.

### Sidebar: Sex as the Confirmation of Polarity

Sex is not recreation. It is not validation. It is not even "intimacy" in its essence. It is the **body's admission of polarity.**

At the **individual level**, sex proves what words cannot: the masculine and feminine currents have recognized their opposites.

- **Her body yields.** This is not consent in the legal sense, nor strategy in the social sense.

Yielding means her vigilance collapses. Her breath deepens. Her hips unlock. The gates of the body obey a law older than choice: "You are axis. I am current. The field demands union."

- **His body claims.** Not through aggression, but through inevitability. His physiology hardens, not from fantasy, but from alignment: "You are chaos. I am structure. The field demands containment."

This is polarity stripped bare: the proof that biology, psychology, and archetype have all recognized the same truth.

### The Error of Modern Men

Most men mistake sex as achievement: proof of charm, wealth, or status. This is illusion. Sex does not validate skill. It validates **field integrity.** If polarity is absent, the act is friction, not confirmation.

### Why Sex Matters in Magnetism

- **Attraction without sex is incomplete.** Desire signals potential polarity.

- **Sex is polarity realized.** The body itself confesses the truth of the field.

- **Post-sex clarity is the verdict.** If polarity was true, she feels rested, opened, reorganized. If polarity was false, she feels emptier, fragmented, ashamed.

The body does not lie. Sex is the verdict of the field.

### The Higher Seal

At the highest level, sex ceases to be personal pleasure. It becomes **ontological testimony**: "The masculine and feminine have recognized and confirmed each other in me."

This is why sex carries weight far beyond the orgasm. It is the most primal sacrament of polarity at the individual level.

### 7. The Seal: Sovereign Eroticism

The ultra magnetic man views sex as alignment, not achievement. He allows lust to arise naturally from polarity, never begging, never manipulating. He knows:

- When he is steady, she will collapse into heat.

- When he is sovereign, she will offer her body.

- When he is axis, she will orbit with desire.

Sex, in this light, is not pursuit. It is **the world's erotic confession** that his field is undeniable.

## Money: The World's Response to Sovereignty

Money does not move toward men who chase it. Money moves toward men whose **field is too steady to ignore.**
The feminine body reads polarity through arousal; the marketplace reads polarity through **sovereignty.**

A man who is clear in direction, immovable in standards, and unapologetic in value becomes a **financial axis**. Investors, clients, partners, allies all re-organize their risk and resources around him, because he provides what most men cannot: a container of inevitability.

### 1. The Feminine Logic of Money

Money mirrors the feminine in its behavior. It circulates, it resists control, it flees neediness, and it yields only to sovereignty. What women test in a man emotionally, money tests in him structurally. The same laws apply—only the channel differs.

- Chase it, and it withdraws.

- Fear losing it, and it punishes you.

- Try to trick it, and it exposes you.

- But stand immovable, declare direction, refuse manipulation—and money **pours toward you.**

The man who understands women but not money is half-magnetic. The man who understands both sees they are the same archetype, mirrored through different channels.

## 2. The Nervous System of Capital

Just as a woman scans your nervous system for leaks, the market scans your life for dissonance. People do not fund your product first—they fund your **presence.**

Money flows where it feels:

- No hidden desperation.

- No nervous collapse under pressure.

- No flinching in refusal.

- No confusion about mission.

To those with resources, need is blood in the water. A man who signals need repels investment. A man who signals sovereignty—even if his numbers are smaller—attracts disproportionate trust.

This is why some men with little proof receive backing, while others with vast resumes starve: money responds not to logic, but to the **embodied aura of stability.**

## 3. Wealth and the Law of Refusal

The highest demonstration of magnetism is not what you accept—it is what you refuse.

Every "yes" reveals your appetite. Every "no" reveals your power. Women test with beauty; money tests with opportunity. Both are asking the same question: "Will you betray yourself for access?"

- A man who cannot walk away from fast money will be enslaved by it.

- A man who refuses misaligned wealth radiates a field that attracts greater wealth.

Money, like women, respects boundaries more than hunger. The paradox: those who need it least, command it most.

## 4. Wealth as Confirmation of Direction

Money follows clarity. Not ambition, not enthusiasm, not hunger—**clarity.**

- A man who knows who he is and where he is going becomes a safer bet than ten men chasing trends.

- A man whose speech is slow, exact, rooted in vision causes investors to calm in his presence.

- A man who can describe his purpose in one line commands more gravity than the one who recites endless credentials.

Wealth is alignment seeking direction. It floods toward those who embody inevitability: "Whether I invest or not, this train will leave the station."

## 5. Archetypal Law: Gold and Kingship

Gold has always circled kings. Not because kings beg for it, but because kings embody **the law of order.**

- The kingdom requires stability, so gold flows where order is present.

- The people crave safety, so resources pool under the axis of clarity.

- The archetypal feminine—symbolized in wealth—offers herself to the masculine archetype of kingship.

This is why wealth without sovereignty destroys men. Lottery winners collapse. Inherited heirs decay. The wealth has no axis to stabilize it, so it becomes poison.

True wealth belongs to the man who can hold it without flinching.

### 6. The Shadow of Wealth Magnetism

The danger of wealth magnetism is greed—the black hole field. The magnetic man must guard against confusing **money's orbit** with **identity**.

- If he begins to chase validation through wealth, he becomes porous.

- If he believes wealth makes him divine, he collapses into tyranny.

- If he fears losing wealth, he broadcasts scarcity and drives it away.

The only posture is sovereignty: wealth is not his god; it is his servant.

## 7. The Seal of Financial Magnetism

The ultra magnetic man never measures himself by his balance sheet. He measures himself by his **refusals, his direction, and his sovereignty.**

Money proves nothing of his worth. It proves only the alignment of his field. When he is steady, wealth pursues him. When he collapses, wealth abandons him.

Thus he remains:

- Axis, not beggar.
- Container, not consumer.
- Sovereign, not slave.

Money is not hunted. It is drawn. It is the world's declaration: "Your presence is safer than mine. Hold this."

### Sidebar: Money as the Confirmation of Sovereignty

Money is not currency. It is **society's confession of who it trusts to hold order.**

At the **societal level**, money is not earned by effort alone. It is pulled toward sovereignty—the man who demonstrates he cannot be bribed, cannot be rushed, cannot be dislodged from his axis.

- **The sovereign man says "no" without collapse.** Money recognizes this as stability.

- **The sovereign man directs without seeking applause.** Money recognizes this as safety.

- **The sovereign man refuses misalignment even at cost.** Money recognizes this as law.

This is why some men with less talent attract more wealth: society would rather entrust resources to a stable axis than to a dazzling instability.

**Wealth is society's vote of confidence in your sovereignty.** It is not proof of genius. It is proof of steadiness.

Chapter 11

# Power: The Collective's Submission to Clarity

Power is not force. Force pushes; power organizes. The truly magnetic man does not "dominate"—he stabilizes the field so completely that others realign themselves around him.

This is the essence of power: **inevitability.** His presence makes alternatives collapse. Enemies orbit him by resisting, allies orbit him by supporting, but all orbit him nonetheless.

### 1. The Archetype of Authority

Every group—whether tribe, company, army, or brotherhood—scans for one signal: "Who can hold the weight of our chaos without collapsing?"

- If no one holds it, the group fragments.

- If a false man pretends to hold it, the group tests him until he cracks.

- If the right man holds it, resistance quiets, loyalties converge, and the collective instinctively defers.

This is not democratic choice. It is archetypal law: **the masculine axis draws submission, the**

**feminine current draws devotion, and together they build hierarchy.**

## 2. Presence as Power

Power begins not in speech, but in silence. A magnetic man enters a room, and the air thickens. People slow down. Jokes shift tone. Men adjust posture. Women check their bodies for arousal or unease.

Why? Because power is a nervous-system transmission. He is not moving faster than others—he is moving slower, heavier, more exact. He is not performing—he is radiating inevitability.

The collective body feels: "Here is the axis. If I resist him, I define myself by him. If I follow him, I find relief in him. Either way, he is central."

## 3. The Law of Speech and Silence

Words either fracture or unify. The powerful man does not speak to fill space; he speaks to collapse uncertainty.

- When he names a direction, the fog clears.

- When he names a boundary, behavior shifts.

- When he names a truth others fear to say, the group exhales.

His silence is weight. His speech is verdict. This is why followers obey not from fear of punishment, but from relief at his clarity.

## 4. Power and the Test of Consequence

No man can hold power without consequence. The group will test him:

- Will he enforce a line, even if it costs him?

- Will he carry responsibility when others collapse?

- Will he pay a personal price to preserve his standard?

When he proves yes, his field hardens. Power consolidates. Men yield loyalty, women yield devotion, even rivals yield respect.

If he fails—if he folds under pressure, avoids consequence, or betrays his own law—his magnetism dissolves. Once dissolved, it is nearly impossible to restore.

## 5. The Shadow of Power

Magnetism at the level of power carries its most dangerous shadow: the intoxication of being central.

- Some men weaponize fear, confusing tyranny for authority.
- Some men mistake orbit for divinity, collapsing into hubris.
- Some men consume their followers for validation, bleeding the very trust that sustained them.

But true power is not ownership. It is stewardship. To forget this is to fall—the inevitable arc of every tyrant who mistook borrowed loyalty for eternal divinity.

## 6. Power as Collective Lust

Just as a woman's body yields to polarity, the collective psyche yields to power. It is not individual desire—it is mass lust for certainty.

- Men lust to be led beyond their own hesitation.

- Women lust to feel their world contained by a force greater than themselves.

- Even enemies lust for the axis—they obsess, they react, they define themselves against him.

In this way, power is the most erotic of currencies. It makes the many yield to the one.

## 7. The Seal of Sovereign Power

The ultra magnetic man remembers:

- Power is not proof of his worth; it is proof of his alignment.

- Power does not belong to him; it flows through him.

- Power is lost the moment he chases it, clings to it, or consumes others for it.

When sovereignty remains intact, power becomes law—not by decree, but by inevitability.

The collective whispers, consciously or not: "Here is the man around whom our chaos can rest. Whether I love him, hate him, follow him, or fight him—I cannot escape him."

That is power.

**Closing the Trinity: Sex, Money, Power**

- **Sex** confirms polarity at the individual level.

- **Money** confirms sovereignty at the societal level.

- **Power** confirms inevitability at the collective level.

But all three are one field. They orbit the same axis. They bend to the same law.

The ultra magnetic man does not chase any of them. He stabilizes himself. He refuses collapse. He maintains sovereignty.

Sex, money, and power then arrive not as prizes—but as **the world's confession** that his field cannot be ignored.

**Sidebar: Power as the Confirmation of Inevitability**

Power is not granted. It is **the collective body reorganizing itself around the man it cannot ignore.**

At the **collective level**, power is the confession of inevitability: "This man resolves our chaos more than he creates it. Therefore, we yield."

- **Followers yield** because his clarity relieves them.

- **Rivals yield** because his axis forces them to define themselves against him.

- **Enemies yield** because their resistance still orbits his centrality.

True power is not commanded. It is recognized. The collective nervous system reads the field and decides unconsciously: "He is the axis. Whether we love or hate him, we organize around him."

This is why history both fears and worships magnetic men. Power is not preference—it is inevitability.

**The Complete Frame**

- **Sex confirms polarity at the individual level.**

- **Money confirms sovereignty at the societal level.**

- **Power confirms inevitability at the collective level.**

Together, they form the trinity of magnetism: the body, the market, and the world all confess the same truth.

Footnote:

**Power**—the deepest of the three. If **Sex** is the body's confession of polarity, and **Money** is the marketplace's confession of sovereignty, then **Power** is the collective's confession of inevitability. This one must be the most weighty—because power is where magnetism either becomes law or becomes corruption.

## Chapter 11

# Brotherhood: The Forge of Magnetism Among Men

A magnetic man is not proven in isolation. Women may yield, money may flow, crowds may admire—but the **final exam of magnetism is how a man holds himself among other men.**

- Women test for polarity.
- Money tests for sovereignty.
- But men test for **truth.**

It is in the gaze of brothers, rivals, and peers that the counterfeit is exposed. No line, no seduction, no performance can survive the relentless calibration of masculine presence against masculine presence.

### 1. Male Hierarchy as a Natural Law

Wherever men gather, a hierarchy emerges—not imposed, but felt. This is not ego, but **the archetypal sorting mechanism of power.**

- Who speaks and others quiet?

- Who absorbs challenge without flinching?

- Who can name the elephant in the room without apology?

The magnetic man does not chase rank, nor does he collapse under it. He accepts the test of hierarchy as natural—just as gravity is natural.

Men yield to clarity, not charm. They follow the one whose nervous system does not leak under pressure, whose standards are sharper than comfort, whose direction relieves them of indecision.

## 2. Brotherhood as a Field of Fire

Women soften men. Brotherhood hardens them.

- The feminine tests through chaos, emotion, and seduction.

- The masculine tests through bluntness, confrontation, and mockery.

Without both, a man is incomplete. The magnetic man **seeks the forge**: brothers who will laugh at his weakness, demand his strength, call out his collapse.

He does not resent correction; he welcomes it. Every challenge absorbed without defense makes his field heavier. Every insult metabolized without collapse makes his gravity denser.

Brotherhood is not comfort—it is the gym of polarity.

### 3. The Law of Male Respect

Among men, respect is not given for charm, beauty, or promises. Respect is given for:

- **Consistency under pressure.** Do you fold when it costs you?

- **Refusals.** Do you betray yourself to gain access—or hold your line?

- **Competence.** Can you deliver what you say, at the level you say?

- **Loyalty.** Do you abandon brothers for advantage—or hold steady?

These four laws are the currency of male respect. Violate them, and magnetism among men collapses, no matter how women respond.

## 4. The Danger of Isolation

Without brotherhood, magnetism rots.

- A man surrounded only by women becomes porous. He begins to need their validation, softening into performance.

- A man surrounded only by money becomes sterile. He begins to worship numbers, mistaking wealth for worth.

- A man surrounded only by followers becomes drunk. He mistakes orbit for divinity, collapsing into tyranny.

Only brothers prevent distortion. They strip away illusion, laugh at delusion, and remind a man that **he is not Source—he is axis.**

## 5. Brotherhood as Transmission of Power

Power multiplies through fraternity. One man can hold a field; ten men aligned can bend reality.

- In battle, brotherhood turns fear into discipline.

- In business, brotherhood turns vision into empire.

- In spirit, brotherhood turns isolation into legacy.

This is why tyrants destroy brotherhood: because men aligned to truth cannot be controlled. And why the wise king cultivates it: because men aligned to truth cannot be overthrown.

## 6. The Seal of Brotherhood

The magnetic man proves himself not only in how women yield or how money flows, but in how **men test him, challenge him, and still trust him.**

He is not above his brothers. He is among them.
He is not needy for them. He is sharpened by them.
He does not fear their challenge. He welcomes it.

Thus his field becomes unbreakable—not because women adored him or crowds applauded him, but because men **forged him.**

# Chapter 12

# The Interior Life of the Magnetic Man

A man may draw women, gather wealth, and command men—yet if his inner axis is hollow, his field collapses when no one is watching.
The foundation of ultra magnetism is not performance in public; it is **sovereignty in solitude.**

The Interior Life is the unseen reservoir from which his presence flows. When women feel safe with him, when money trusts him, when men respect him—it is because, beneath the noise, he is already tethered to **something greater than himself.**

### 1. Solitude as Source

Many people in general fear silence. Left alone, they seek distraction, stimulation, validation. This restlessness is felt by others as leakage: the subtle need to be filled.

---

Footnote: **Interior Life** —this is where the ultra magnetic man roots his power beyond women, money, and men. Without this interior axis, all other magnetism is temporary seduction.

The magnetic man does not fear solitude; he cultivates it. He knows that silence is not emptiness, but **the womb of power.** In solitude:

- His nervous system unwinds from external hooks.

- His aim clarifies without interference.

- His energy resets to sovereignty, rather than performance.

Solitude is not escape—it is calibration. Every public field is anchored in private silence.

## 2. The Relationship to Death

Every man's magnetism is capped by his fear of death. A man terrified of loss, decline, or mortality leaks desperation in every pursuit. Women feel it as neediness. Money feels it as greed. Men feel it as insecurity.

The magnetic man meditates on death—not morbidly, but soberly. He carries in his posture the law: "All this ends. Therefore I am free."

This freedom makes him untouchable:

- He cannot be bribed—because he does not fear loss.

- He cannot be seduced—because he does not cling.
- He cannot be dominated—because he does not dread endings.

His field radiates inevitability because he has already reconciled with the ultimate inevitability.

## 3. The Metabolism of Suffering

Life breaks men. But suffering does not destroy magnetism; it refines it.

Weak men resist pain, complain about pain, or mask pain. Their suffering leaks outward, burdening others.
Magnetic men **metabolize pain.** They feel it fully, let it burn, and allow it to deepen their stillness.

This is why women trust them with vulnerability, why men respect their gravity, why money flows to their stability: others sense "This man has carried weight and not collapsed. Therefore he can carry mine."

The more suffering a man has metabolized without leaking, the denser his gravity becomes.

## 4. Alignment with the Divine

At the root of every magnetic man is a tether to something higher. Call it God, Source, the Absolute—it is not religion, it is alignment.

- Without it, a man believes he is Source, and collapses into tyranny.
- With it, he becomes a vessel—his power is not his, but borrowed.

This alignment is what keeps magnetism clean. It reminds him:

- Sex is holy, not hunger.
- Money is service, not status.
- Power is stewardship, not ownership.

The magnetic man kneels in private so he can stand in public.

## 5. Daily Rituals of the Interior Axis

The interior life is not philosophy—it is practice.

- **Silence:** time each day with no input, no device, no stimulation.

- **Reflection:** honest confrontation with where he leaked, where he folded, where he betrayed himself.

- **Invocation:** a return to Source, whether through prayer, meditation, or contemplation of the Absolute.

- **Embodiment:** training the body not for vanity, but for discipline—proof that will directs flesh.

These rituals are not optional—they are maintenance of sovereignty. Without them, the field corrodes.

## 6. The Seal of the Interior Man

The ultra magnetic man is not defined by women, money, or followers. He is defined by what happens in his silence.

He has made peace with solitude.
He has befriended death.
He has metabolized pain.
He has tethered himself to the Absolute.

Therefore, when he enters a room, others feel not just a man—but a field rooted in eternity.

That is why his magnetism does not fade when trends shift, when wealth fluctuates, when crowds disperse. It endures—because it is not anchored in them, but in the **unseen axis within him.**

# Chapter 13

# Legacy: The Continuance of the Magnetic Field

Sex confirms polarity.
Money confirms sovereignty.
Power confirms inevitability.
But **Legacy** confirms immortality.

Every magnetic man eventually leaves the room. His body ages. His wealth shifts. His power is tested. The question is: does his field vanish with him, or does it remain after he is gone?

Legacy is magnetism extended across time. It is when a man's clarity, law, and axis are transmitted so deeply into others that his absence does not collapse the order—because his presence has become a pattern embedded in them.

**1. Legacy as Field-Imprint**

Magnetism is not just energy in the moment—it is an imprint in the nervous systems of others.

- A woman who has been truly claimed will carry that calibration even when she leaves. She will compare every man after him to his axis.

- Men who have been forged by his presence will hear his voice in their decisions, even when he is not there.

- Communities he has touched will organize themselves around principles he demonstrated, not slogans he preached.

This is field-imprint: the invisible architecture left behind by his gravity.

## 2. Transmission Through Brotherhood

Legacy does not survive through followers; it survives through brothers. Followers imitate; brothers inherit.

- A follower quotes your words.

- A brother embodies your standard.

- A follower needs you present.

- A brother carries your absence like a banner.

This is why true legacy requires **initiation**—not just teaching, but testing, challenging, and forging others until they embody your clarity themselves.

Legacy begins the moment a man stops asking, "How many can I attract?" and starts asking, "Who can I forge to stand when I am gone?"

### 3. Woman as Legacy-Carrier

The feminine, too, carries legacy. When a magnetic man impregnates a woman—whether biologically with children or energetically with calibration—she becomes a vessel of his field.

- Biologically, his bloodline transmits not just DNA, but the embodied pattern of sovereignty.

- Spiritually, women who have rested in his axis cannot forget it. They become, in their own way, evangelists of his presence—often unconsciously.

Thus legacy is carried not only through men who rise in his image, but through women whose bodies and psyches were transformed by his gravity.

### 4. The Archetypal Law of Continuance

Every archetype seeks perpetuation. Kingship is incomplete if it dies with the king. Brotherhood is incomplete if it dies with the band. Magnetism is incomplete if it dies with the man.

The archetypal law is this: **true sovereignty replicates itself.**

- The magnetic man without legacy is a flame that burned but left no light behind.

- The magnetic man with legacy is a fire whose heat is felt for generations.

## 5. The Shadow of Legacy

The pursuit of legacy is dangerous. Many men attempt to **force immortality** through monuments, wealth-hoarding, or reputation-chasing. These do not last.

- Monuments crumble.

- Wealth dissipates.

- Names are forgotten.

Only the **field itself** remains—how others' nervous systems were reorganized in his presence. If he taught them dependence, his legacy rots. If he taught them sovereignty, his legacy multiplies.

The shadow is ego; the antidote is transmission.

**Sidebar:**
The shadow of magnetism always collapses into ego. Ego makes the field about self — seeking validation, performing for attention, hoarding energy. This inversion turns magnetism into hunger.

The antidote is transmission. Transmission means the self becomes a conduit for essence, not a consumer of energy. Instead of pulling for approval, the magnetic being radiates signal. Instead of grasping, they give. Instead of collapsing others into their need, they expand others through their overflow.

Ego says, "See me."
Transmission says, "Here is the signal."

This is the law: ego corrupts magnetism into costume; transmission purifies magnetism into inevitability.

## 6. The Seal of Legacy

The ultra magnetic man lives with the awareness that death is certain—but collapse is optional.

He knows:

- Sex will fade, but the women he awakened will never forget the axis.

- Money will pass, but those who trusted him will replicate his standard.

- Power will shift, but the men he forged will embody his law.

His legacy is not his possessions, nor his reputation, but the **continuance of his field** in others.

When he is gone, people will still organize by his standard, still feel his calibration, still yield to his axis. This is immortality—not of flesh, but of field.

# Chapter 14

# THE SOVEREIGN ARCHETYPE:

### *The Blueprint for Irreversible Masculine Magnetism, Wealth Recursion, and Energetic Superiority*

"The field responds not to effort, nor charisma, nor desire — but to structural inevitability. Magnetism is not charm. It is cosmic authority made visible."

### I. THE MALE VOID: THE SPACE THAT COMMANDS

True masculine magnetism is not a personality trait — it is the **presence of an energetic void** that exerts structural gravity on everything around it.

Whereas the feminine expands to attract, the **masculine contracts to command**. This contraction is not repression. It is **containment** — the sacred capacity to **refuse reaction, refuse leaking**, and hold **coherent density of will** in a field full of chaos.

The magnetic man does **not pull attention** — he **collapses possibility**. In his presence, lesser timelines die. Choices reduce. The world simplifies. His presence **does not offer options** — it presents **inevitability**.

This is why most men fail. They are still trying to be liked. Still trying to be chosen. Still trying to prove. The ultra magnetic man has **eliminated the need for external validation** because he understands that true magnetism is not the result of being wanted — it is the **byproduct of being inevitable**.

## II. THE THREE STRUCTURAL FIELDS OF MASCULINE DOMINANCE

All external manifestations — money, sex, status, control — obey three internal fields. Until these are **set into recursive integrity**, no amount of action will matter.

### 1. The Recursive Field of Power (Will)

This is the **core generator**. Not ambition. Not hope. But **unified internal recursion** of identity, desire, and consequence.
You do not act and then become — you **become, and then everything must act in response**.

If your inner structure doesn't contain your own energy, it cannot command others.

This field is built by:

- Unifying all personal contradictions.
- Severing external approval dependencies.
- Choosing the path of total alignment even when it guarantees isolation, rejection, or confrontation — and refusing to dilute your signal to survive.

## 2. The Structural Field of Command (Presence)

This is not emotional control. It is **energetic stillness**.

### A man cannot lead what he cannot quiet

Leadership begins not with action but with resonance. If your internal field is noisy — reactive, insecure, scattered — you will amplify chaos in others, not direction. To quiet something is to bring it into harmonic coherence. If you cannot bring order to the emotional field around you (or within you), then what follows you is not loyalty — it's confusion.

**A man cannot own what he cannot slow**

Ownership is not control through speed or dominance. It is anchoring. What you cannot decelerate — whether it's a decision, a woman, a conflict, or your own thoughts — is evidence that your energetic field lacks mass. True ownership means your presence slows the entropy of a system and brings it into your rhythm.

**A man cannot magnetize what he cannot stabilize**

Attraction without containment is collapse. If you pull energy, people, or power toward you — but cannot hold it in coherent form — it will destabilize, repel, or turn against you. Stabilization means you are not shaken by what you draw in. You do not leak, panic, or shift. You become the still point that all else orbits.

Presence is the ability to **collapse the emotional wave** before it is broadcast — so the world responds to **your structure**, not your reaction.

### 3. The Field of Prophetic Design (Vision)

**Men who have not decoded their inner architecture are forced to borrow meaning from outer noise.**
They follow trends, copy content, mimic success

formulas, or join movements not because they are inspired — but because they are lost. This is not stupidity. It is structural absence. When a man has not located the cosmic geometry of his being — the exact signature he was encoded to express — he will latch onto temporary maps created by other men.

**The magnetic man has unearthed his original recursion pattern — the blueprint that governs his existence beyond biography.**
This is not about his job title, his industry, or even his passions. Those are outer wrappers. His true mission is the **energetic transmission he was built to make inevitable on Earth**, regardless of medium or method. It is a structural signature, not a career path.

**This is why he does not chase opportunities — he magnetizes alignment.**
He is not wondering what to do next, where to go, or who to follow. His inner pattern becomes a living gravity that draws every external event into precision sync with the recursion he has activated.

He sees himself **as a structural recursion** of cosmic force on Earth. Every movement, investment, conversation, and posture **expresses the higher order** of this recursion.

This is why he **cannot be replaced**. You cannot replace an **irreplaceable pattern**.

## III. THE SEED VAULT: MASCULINE ENERGY AS CURRENCY

Most men hemorrhage power by **misusing their seed** — not only sexually, but across all dimensions of energetic distribution.
The magnetic male **does not "retain" by force** — he retains because he is **unwilling to allow extraction** without **energetic equalization**.

This includes:

- Conversations that do not reciprocate value.

- Sexual encounters that do not **build the masculine field**.

- Business engagements that distort or delay his recursion flow.

He is not "guarded." He is **consecrated**.

Where the average man gives his energy for attention, the ultra magnetic male gives **nothing** that does not **expand his sovereignty**.

## IV. THE MAGNETIC ENGINE: WEALTH WITHOUT NEED

The world is not attracted to men who need money — it is attracted to men who **do not need money but generate it anyway**.

Why? Because money obeys recursion.

- Men who **need** money disrupt the field with anxiety.

- Men who **deserve** money broadcast entitlement.

- But men who are **structurally aligned with wealth** cause money to **obey**, because they have **collapsed all contradiction** between inner and outer value.

The ultra magnetic male does not "chase" money — he **builds structures that money cannot escape**.

These structures:

- Provide value through **energetic uniqueness**, not imitation.

- Operate on **asymmetrical leverage** (1 action = 1000x return).

- Are built to **function without needing validation**, applause, or saving the world.

His money comes from being **a vortex**, not an employee of effort.

## V. SEXUAL FIELD COMMAND: THE FINAL SEAL

All sexual magnetism flows through **field containment**.

What seduces the feminine is not surface. It is **what she cannot shake** — his **certainty**, **composure**, and **coherence**, even when she tests, withdraws, or erupts.

His sexual energy is not used to chase — it is used to **bind timelines, fracture illusions**, and **embed memory**. He becomes **a recursive landmark** in her nervous system — not because he played a role, but because he **embodied a structural reality** she had never touched before.

And **she knows**: if she cannot rise to match it, she will be expelled by it.

This is not cruelty. This is recursion law.

## VI. THE REAL-WORLD VORTEX: HOW IT LOOKS

You will know him not by his outfit, words, or even confidence — but by his **uninterruptibility**.

He walks into a room and the room orients.
He speaks, and silence follows.
He says little, because **he has nothing to prove**.
People feel the pull but cannot name it.
Women orbit.
Men adjust.
Time slows.
And even when he walks away, his absence **feels more present** than most people's presence.

He is **not a performer**.
He is **not a player**.
He is **not a prophet**.

He is the **masculine recursion made flesh** — and the world does not choose him.
It **yields**.

## VII. FINAL TRANSMISSION

The Ultra Magnetic Male does not win because he is smarter, louder, or more charming.

He wins because **there is no alternative to him**.

He has become the **structural inevitability** of power, sex, wealth, and direction — and in a collapsing world, he is the **only architecture that still holds**.

While others seek to be seen,
He becomes the **frame** through which the world sees.

And that...
cannot be bought, faked, taught, or stolen.

It must be **forged**.

And once forged,
**The world must follow.**

# Chapter 15

# THE KING FREQUENCY

WHAT IS KING FREQUENCY?

King Frequency is not an attitude.
It is not a style.
It is not about being dominant, desirable, or successful.

**It is a metaphysical field**—a precise energetic configuration of structure, law, and divine embodiment that makes a man unfuckwithable at the core. A man seated in King Frequency is not "acting like a king." He has become the governing axis of his own domain. He is the stabilizing force that other beings subconsciously orbit, not because he demands obedience—but because **his field is coded to command it**.

A king is not seeking approval.
He is not seeking women.
He is not even seeking power.

He is carrying **law**—and the world adjusts around it.

## The Field of the Throne

At its core, **King Frequency is a regulatory force.**
It is the internal electromagnetic pattern that:

- Governs the man's nervous system
- Stabilizes the emotional storms of others
- Anchors the polarity between chaos and order
- Imposes no external force—but radiates a non-negotiable axis

The King does not rise by dominance. He remains by law.
He governs **through calibration, not conquest**. Women, men, money, and meaning respond not to his words, but to the geometry of his being.

The King is not playing chess. He is the board.

## Masculine Throne vs Masculine Performance

There are two kinds of men:

1. The **performer**, who postures and contorts to appear strong.

2. The **king**, whose silence does more than the performer's loudest hour.

The performer uses:

- Charisma to overcompensate for internal instability

- Spiritual language to fake alignment

- Aggression to mask internal collapse

- Female attention to pretend he's valuable

But the King...

- Speaks when there is something real to transmit

- Looks straight through performance because he has no need to mirror it

- Does not need to be respected—because he already governs himself

Where the performer seeks external proof, the King operates from **internal proof-of-work**. The throne is not built on perception—it is built on the integrity of the structure underneath.

## "King Frequency is a Burden—Not a Boost"

Let it be clear:

**The throne is not a perk of masculinity. It is a burden of alignment.**

The man who walks in King Frequency does not get to collapse when it's hard. He does not get to leak energy when seduced. He does not get to default to logic when her storm arrives. He does not get to chase validation when leadership becomes lonely.

King Frequency is not a title. It is a **spiritual furnace**. It either burns away the false self or forges an indestructible one.

## "King Frequency is Not a Crown You Wear — It's a Code You Maintain"

Every day the King wakes up, he faces one test:

"Can I hold the throne today?"
"Can I regulate my frame when others collapse?"
"Can I speak with clarity when others manipulate?"
"Can I govern my sexual charge instead of leaking it?"

"Can I move in mission without applause?"
"Can I protect without attachment, lead without control, love without dependency?"

There is no arrival.
There is only **maintenance of alignment.**

The throne **is not a possession**.
It is a **living contract** between the man and the divine masculine architecture within him.

## "Women Do Not Respond to You — They Respond to the Throne"

When a man activates King Frequency, he notices a shift:

- He does less — but creates more gravity

- He says less — but his presence is remembered

- He doesn't seduce — but feminine energy leans in

- He doesn't chase — but becomes the axis around which others orient

Why? Because the King does not offer attraction.
**He offers reality**.

And the feminine, when confronted with real structure, either surrenders, flees, or tests. But it always responds.

**The Core of King Frequency**

Let us define it clearly.

**King Frequency is the fusion of energetic sovereignty, nervous system regulation, structural integrity, and directional clarity—without seeking permission.**

It is:

- The ability to hold pain without folding
- The ability to hold beauty without leaking
- The ability to hold polarity without collapsing
- The ability to hold truth without persuading

It is not a style—it is a signal.
It is not a performance—it is a posture.
It is not an emotion—it is a structure.

Let this be the foundation of the throne.

When you walk in a room, King Frequency means:

"My field already knows who I am.
Your recognition is optional."

That is where we begin.

# THE INNER ARCHITECTURE OF THE THRONE

## The Four Pillars That Sustain the King Field

The King is not a role—it is a **system of inner structures** that maintains its own gravitational consistency, even in chaos. Without these structures, a man may temporarily imitate the crown, but he cannot **hold the weight of it**.

There are **four non-negotiable pillars** that govern the metaphysical throne. If even one collapses, the entire field is compromised:

## 1. Energetic Sovereignty

**Definition:** The man has full ownership over his life force, sexual energy, emotional charge, and thought field.

He is not borrowed. He is not leaky. He is not outsourced.

- His energy is not hijacked by praise or destroyed by insult.

- His sexual force is contained and directed, not scattered or baited.

- His focus is not subject to impulse, distraction, or external nervous systems.

**Real World Markers:**

- Women feel safe around him without knowing why.

- Men respect him without needing to agree with him.

- No one feels they can "pull him off center."

**Diagnostic Line:**

"If your energy can be hijacked, the throne was never yours."

## 2. Nervous System Regulation

**Definition:** The man's nervous system is the **anchor**, not the amplifier, of the environment.

He does not escalate tension. He does not avoid it. He becomes the container that grounds it.

- In conflict: he responds from clarity, not reaction.

- In beauty: he receives without leaking or simping.

- In chaos: he slows time, not just thought.

The throne is nervous system architecture. Without regulation, the "king" becomes an emotional adolescent with a crown.

**Real World Markers:**

- His presence diffuses chaos, not through effort—but through energetic law.

- Women test him emotionally—and instinctively trust him more when he doesn't flinch.

- Others feel "time slows down" when he speaks.

**Diagnostic Line:**

"If you can't stabilize others without suppressing yourself—you are not yet throne-calibrated."

## 3. Structural Integrity

**Definition:** The man's actions, words, habits, values, and private conduct are **unified**—with no internal contradiction.

He is not divided between public power and private collapse.
He is not one man in front of her, another man alone in the dark.

- If he says it—he does it.
- If he feels it—he owns it.
- If he wants it—he moves toward it.

He does not chase alignment. He lives in it.

**Real World Markers:**

- A woman knows exactly where she stands with him—because he doesn't need games.
- Other men may challenge him—but cannot expose him.
- Life tests him—and he remains whole under pressure.

**Diagnostic Line:**

"If you are hiding any part of your identity—then your field is fragmented. Fragmentation cannot govern."

## 4. Directional Clarity

**Definition:** The man is calibrated to **higher instruction**, not just ambition.

He knows where he is going—and why.
He is not wandering in search of validation, status, sex, or safety.
He is moving toward a non-negotiable transmission of purpose.

The King is not just building a life. He is embodying a blueprint from the infinite—and structuring it on Earth.

**Real World Markers:**

- He doesn't speak vision for attention—he moves as if **watched by God**.

- He does not rely on external motivation.

- His movement cuts through confusion—not by force, but by resonance.

## Diagnostic Line:

"If your path requires applause, you are still lost. The King path is encoded—not externally assigned."

## Summary Grid: The Four Pillars of the Throne

| Pillar | Meaning | Collapse Sign | Activation Sign |
|---|---|---|---|
| Energetic Sovereignty | Ownership of life force and field | Leaky focus, seduction vulnerability, overstimulation | Others feel "containment" in your presence |
| Nervous System Regulation | Anchor under pressure | Emotional spikes, collapse under beauty or conflict | Storms calm in your field |
| Structural Integrity | Whole alignment of word, habit, value, behavior | Inconsistencies, performative morality, hidden vices | Trust is felt without needing explanation |
| Directional Clarity | Divine assignment over external ambition | Seeking meaning, reactive purpose, impulsive pivots | Moves as if monitored by higher law |

A man who calibrates these four pillars **becomes unshakable**.

The room listens when he breathes.
The feminine opens without knowing why.
The storm tests him—but finds no entry point.

He does not yell. He does not posture. He does not explain.
He simply **holds the axis.**

## Chapter 15

# SEVEN PILLARS OF KING FREQUENCY

The Inner Throne Revealed from the Inside Out

### 1. Unshakeable Nervous System

The masculine nervous system is the throne room of polarity.

When it is scattered, erratic, or emotionally entangled, the man becomes collapsible — reactive to the woman's wave, susceptible to mimicry, and enslaved to stimulus. But when his nervous system is sealed, grounded, and voltage-regulated, he becomes immovable without becoming numb, sensitive without being chaotic, and aware without needing to explain.

An unshakeable nervous system is not one that avoids pressure — it **invites pressure** and refuses to contort. This is the **energetic stabilizer** that holds its axis while being tested by chaos, lust, disappointment, or feminine emotional heat.

If the woman's storm destabilizes him, he is not ready.
If the world's resistance derails him, he is still in apprenticeship.
The King breathes through fire — and **his breath is law**.

## 2. Energetic Boundaries Without Collapse

A King does not explain his boundaries — his field is the boundary.

He is not protecting himself from the feminine. He is protecting her from his own instability, and protecting the divine order from being inverted.

His "no" is not an act of rejection. It is the **architecture of masculine intelligence** — the part that regulates rhythm, guards sanctity, and establishes polarity.

He does not collapse into over-accommodation, performative approval, or spiritual bypassing. Nor does he swing into rigidity, punishment, or dissociation. His boundaries are **living geometry** — shaped by clarity, not fear.

A woman feels it before he speaks:

"I am free to express myself in this man's presence, but I cannot manipulate it.
I am welcome to open, but I cannot destabilize his axis."


## 3. No Need to Perform or Persuade

The counterfeit masculine seeks to **convince**.
The King simply **is**.

He is not constructing an identity through spiritual lingo, financial signals, alpha mimicry, or wounded emotional transparency. He is not building a castle of commentary around his unhealed ache.

The true masculine throne **does not chase approval, likes, reactions, or seduction results** — it sits in silence and **lets presence do the sorting**.

This is the man who does not try to win her mind —

He holds his own and lets her alignment or departure reveal the truth.

To persuade is to posture.
To perform is to doubt your own throne.
The King does neither.

## 4. Silent Motion and Precision of Direction

A King moves like a man whose future is already written.

He does not hustle to explain, overshare his vision, or perform ambition.
He does not breadcrumb plans to appear powerful or conscious.

He walks in **precise silence** — a silence that is **so full of encoded direction**, it calibrates others in its presence.

This is not stoicism or withdrawal — it is **surgical sovereignty**.

His motion is not reactive to the feminine's wave.
His vision is not edited by outer applause.
His pace is not disturbed by the delay of outcome.

He has already decided what his life is for — and the woman either **joins the current** or **respects the mission's boundary**.

## 5. Clear Desire Without Chasing or Leakage

The King is **not neutered**.
He wants. He desires. He **hungers**.

But he never leaks that hunger into performance, desperation, seduction, or compromise. He makes his desire known — raw, clear, simple — and never weaponizes it for access or identity.

He does not pretend he's detached.
He does not shrink his passion.
But neither does he negotiate with polarity to be chosen.

He says without flinch:

"I want you. I don't need you."
"I offer access, not pursuit."
"I initiate with clarity — not collapse."

And because his energy is **directional**, not entangled, it activates the feminine to **self-select into truth**.

### 6. Soul-Coded Purpose, Not Persona

The King is not building an identity.
He is building a **legacy from the blueprint of his soul**.

He is not a mirror of trending ideologies, social roles, or trauma adaptations. His life is not governed by optics — it is **devoted to assignment**.

Purpose is not performance.
It is not about scale, status, or followers.
It is **alignment to Source** through obedience to the internal command.

He does not say "I want to be a leader."
He simply leads.

He does not chase meaning.
He lives in such congruence that everything becomes meaningful.

She feels this — not in his words, but in his architecture:

"This man is already building a kingdom.
If I enter his field, I am entering a current that will shape my soul."

## 7. Truth as Law, Not as Debate

The final test: can he **stand in truth without flinching** — even if it means rejection?

The counterfeit masculine negotiates.
The wounded masculine deflects.
The King speaks truth **as law**, not as dialogue.

Not cruel. Not arrogant. Not rigid.
But non-negotiable in alignment.

He says what is true —
Even when it costs the woman's desire.
Even when it ends the performance.
Even when silence would keep her interest longer.

"This is what I see."
"This is where I stand."
"This is what I will not compromise."

And in doing so, he becomes **worthy of trust**,
even if not always understood.

## "Women Feel When You're On Code"

When a man is truly seated on the throne — not performing masculinity, not echoing dominance, not cosplaying leadership — but **anchored in his internal law**... the feminine does not "choose" him in the conventional sense.

She **responds involuntarily**, magnetically, and structurally.

This is not emotional attraction.
It is **nervous system submission to stability**.

A magnetic woman doesn't "fall in love" with a King — she **falls under law**.
His frequency holds a voltage she cannot debate.
She can either **collapse into it**, or flee from it — but she **cannot ignore it**.

## No Chase — Just Collapse:

She doesn't pursue him, test him, or need to extract proof from him.
She simply feels safe **collapsing her nervous system** into his — not because he seduced her, but because his architecture rendered manipulation unnecessary.

She is not analyzing him.
She is **being revealed** by him.
His presence is **a mirror**, and in that mirror she sees her own polarity activated.

This is not about dominance.
It is about **energetic justice**.

## No Seduction — Just Recognition:

She opens not because of charm, strategy, or scripts.
She opens because she **recognizes the throne** — the invisible code of structure, self-regulation, purpose, and clarity that no words can fake.

"She opens not because you seduced her —
but because she saw the throne within you
and chose to kneel in recognition."

Her submission is not performative.
It is **visceral**.
It is the body recognizing alignment, the psyche surrendering to sovereignty, the soul remembering the original pattern of sacred polarity.

Chapter 15

## This Is Divine Structural Alignment:

In King Frequency, he does not perform power — he simply **withholds collapse**.
He does not demand her surrender — he simply **removes volatility from his field**.
And in doing so, he creates a **safe architecture for her full expression**.

When she tests him, she is testing for collapse — not for dominance.
When she withdraws, she is measuring the **depth of his presence** — not seeking punishment.

The woman becomes a barometer, not an obstacle. Her polarity **reveals the strength** of his internal order.

And when he passes these invisible tests, not through aggression, but through **spiritual gravity**, she doesn't just lean in — she **lets go of control**.

## KINGS & COLLAPSE PATTERNS

### (How the Masculine Mimics the Throne But Cannot Hold It)

The King Frequency cannot be mimicked. It can only be forged.
But in a world where perception outweighs precision, many men wear imitation crowns — energetic costumes built on performance, validation-seeking, or avoidance of responsibility.

These men are not always wicked.
But they are unstable.
And when a man masquerades as a king without the nervous system to hold divine weight, he creates spiritual damage — to himself, to the feminine, and to the ecosystem of polarity.

False kings seduce through projection.
True kings stabilize through presence.
This is not about status. It's about structure.

Below are the **five counterfeit archetypes** of masculine collapse — and the throne frequencies they violate.

Chapter 15

## 1. The Crown Without Gravity

"He looks like a leader, but his field is empty."

This man projects confidence but lacks interior resonance.
He borrows the language of power — but cannot channel the force.
He may attract attention, build audiences, or be seen as a visionary... but his energy is hollow.

- **Traits:**
  - Speaks well but feels light
  - Uses spiritual or leadership language without embodiment
  - Evaporates under pressure
  - Energetically needs recognition to feel worthy

- **Collapse Pattern:**
  This man builds castles without a foundation.
  He attracts admiration, even devotion, but cannot stabilize the women or men around him.
  His frequency cannot hold weight — so when responsibility arrives, he defaults to avoidance, performance, or blame.

- **Law Broken:**
  **Presence without grounding is not power — it is theater.**
  He violates the throne frequency of unshakeable nervous system and truth as law.

## 2. The Alpha Mimic

"He confuses dominance with divinity."

This man leads by force, not by frame.
He postures aggressively, demands submission, and often builds his identity on seduction or status — not structure.

- **Traits:**
  - Relies on intimidation, seduction, or competition
  - Attracts women through fear or control
  - Seeks to be obeyed, not recognized
  - Triggers collapse in feminine nervous systems

- **Collapse Pattern:**
  He seems confident until challenged by an equal — especially a woman who sees

through the performance.
His "strength" is armor. His reactions expose his fragility.
He becomes erratic, cruel, or disappears when he cannot dominate the room.

- **Law Broken:**
  **If you require submission to feel masculine, you are not a king — you are a tyrant.**
  He violates the throne frequency of energetic boundaries without collapse and silent precision of direction.

### 3. The Spiritual Performer

"He weaponizes wisdom he hasn't earned."

This man speaks like an initiate but lives like an echo.
He has mastered sacred language, ritual aesthetics, and emotional transparency — but none of it is seated in sovereignty.

- **Traits:**
    - Uses spiritual language to seduce or validate

- Performs vulnerability but collapses under accountability
- Avoids hard truths by over-communicating emotionally
- Leaks sexual or energetic boundaries under the guise of "depth"

- **Collapse Pattern:**
  He draws in high-value, conscious women who seek sacred masculinity — but leaves them destabilized.
  His "wisdom" dissolves when he is not praised.
  His inner throne has no law, only longing.

- **Law Broken:**
  **If your masculinity dissolves without admiration, it was never sacred — it was sales.**
  He violates the throne frequency of soul-coded purpose and truth as law.

## 4. The Helper King

"He confuses being needed with being worthy."

This man derives identity from being useful, needed, or "the safe space."
He over-gives. He over-functions. He stabilizes others while secretly destabilizing himself.

- **Traits:**
    - Acts as therapist, fixer, or emotional rescuer
    - Avoids conflict to preserve connection
    - Believes love is earned through sacrifice
    - Suffocates polarity by becoming energetically feminine
- **Collapse Pattern:**
  He unconsciously selects partners who need healing — not because of compassion, but because he cannot hold sovereignty without being validated through service. When a woman grows or no longer needs him, he implodes emotionally or turns passive-aggressive.

- **Law Broken:**
  **If you only feel powerful when others are broken — you are not a king. You are a crutch.**
  He violates the throne frequency of clear desire without leakage and presence without performance.

### 5. The Eternal Initiate

"He is always evolving — but never arriving."

This man is deeply spiritual, self-aware, and constantly "doing the work" — but uses transformation as a hiding place.

- **Traits:**
    - Obsessed with healing, shadow work, or not being "ready"
    - Fears claiming space, power, or leadership
    - Discards relationships when too much responsibility appears
    - Hides behind humility to avoid full embodiment

## Chapter 15

- **Collapse Pattern:**
  His growth becomes an identity — and identity becomes avoidance.
  He is allergic to crown space.
  Anytime a moment of true power or leadership arises, he sabotages it and returns to the comfort of becoming.

- **Law Broken:**
  **If your transformation never produces action, your soul is hiding.**
  He violates the throne frequency of purpose as law and structure as embodiment.

**Final Law:**

**The throne is not earned through language, light, or likes.
It is revealed by who remains seated when everything collapses.**

Any man can decorate the temple.
Only the King holds the gravitational field that stabilizes it.
And it is not presence alone that makes him holy — it is law.

## Throne is Not Given — It is Maintained

*"King Frequency is not an achievement. It is a discipline."*

### The Throne as a Living Geometry:

The throne is not a metaphor. It is a **metaphysical structure** — a living geometry that responds to coherence, collapses under chaos, and calibrates itself to the laws the man keeps. A man does not "own" the throne just because he once embodied strength or made a woman melt. The throne is **not gifted through attraction**, it is **earned through alignment**— and **maintained through unwavering discipline** in multiple domains of Self.

A man may be crowned once. But if he does not stabilize the frequency, **the crown will rot on his head.**

### Stability is Sovereignty:

**Stability** is the masculine's most sacred offering. Not emotional numbness. Not passive neutrality. But a nervous system, mind, and spirit that **refuse to collapse** under pressure. A woman tests this — not because she wants drama, but because she needs to know whether the throne can **carry the weight of life**, not just seduction.

The King does not fear this pressure. He is pressure.
He does not chase alignment — he **issues law** through his presence.

He does not lead through dominance — he **embodies structure** that evokes surrender.
And he knows: if his presence is shaky, **nothing else he builds will hold.**

**What He Must Stabilize — Daily, Relentlessly:**

**1. His Thoughts**
The King is not owned by thought loops, projections, or inner noise. He disciplines the mind **before it becomes a narrative**. He watches for fantasy, egoic indulgence, or cycles of self-betrayal. He does not let his thoughts spin unguarded — he **holds them to account like a court of law.**

He does not speak every thought. He sanctifies the ones that deserve life.

**2. His Mission**
Mission is not ambition. It is not productivity. The King holds a **soul-bound trajectory** that transcends momentary feelings. Even when tired,

triggered, distracted — he realigns with his path. If the world rejects him, if the woman misreads him — he doesn't spiral.

He remembers the flame that no one else sees, and he walks toward it anyway.

### 3. His Frequency

The throne is not how he feels. It's what he **emits when no one is watching**. His frequency is his inner field — structured, clear, masculine in polarity. It is not scattered, leaky, or desperate for feedback.

He clears static by:

- Closing loops (no open-ended confusion)

- Protecting his word (no energetic bleeding)

- Resetting quickly after misalignment

The throne is maintained by energetic law — not mood.

### 4. His Woman

If he holds a woman in his field, he holds her without control. He doesn't collapse into her chaos, nor does he dominate her submission. He does not lead through words — he leads through **felt presence**. He makes no promises he won't enforce. He does not ask for trust — he becomes **trust in form**.

She doesn't follow him because he says the right things.
She follows him because she can feel: nothing in him is pretending.

## The Law of Maintenance: Presence Over Peaks

A counterfeit king peaks early. He seduces with a burst of clarity, collapses into confusion, then blames her for withdrawing. The real king is **slow fire**. He does not need to spike to impress. He sustains the field by **living the law in silence**.

- No energy is ever wasted defending his role.

- No flattery is needed to be received.

- No test shakes him — because he expects them, welcomes them, and reflects back reality.

It's not dominance — it's density. His throne is a gravitational field.

## Maintenance Is a Daily Jurisdiction:

The King does not "hold frame" for the moment. He governs an **entire psychic kingdom** — his body, thoughts, woman, mission, finances, lineage, and legacy.

And he knows: every time he leaks, lies, or hesitates, he forfeits law.
So he corrects quickly. Not perfectly — but lawfully.

- He does not ghost his purpose.

- He does not ghost his woman.

- He does not ghost himself.

The throne is not held by perfection. It is held by principle.

## Final Law: No Law, No Crown

The crown is forged by fire — but **it is secured through law**.
The moment a man forfeits the law, the throne begins to rot.

- Law of speech

- Law of direction

- Law of containment

- Law of presence

- Law of restraint

- Law of action

- Law of return

If a man governs these daily — **he need not perform, pursue, or persuade.**
The throne will govern for him.

No law, no crown.
No structure, no trust.
No consistency, no kingdom.

**Woman**

# Chapter 16

# The Ultra-Magnetic Woman I

To embody an ultra-magnetic feminine field — one capable of drawing men, resources, and destiny with inevitability — a woman must understand: her magnetism is not cosmetics, charm, or seduction. It is the field-result of **energetic receptivity fused with sovereign containment.**

Where the ultra-magnetic man is axis, the ultra-magnetic woman is **field.** He bends reality through coherence — by emitting a singular, unwavering directive from his being. She bends reality through **charged openness** — by receiving energy into herself without losing her internal axis or dissolving her form.

Her magnetism is not in her emotionality — but in her capacity to absorb intensity while remaining rooted in her own energetic shape.

**Sidebar:**

**KEY METAPHYSICAL CLARIFICATIONS**

**"Charged Openness" — What Is It?**
This refers to the feminine's ability to **stay open, responsive, and emotionally available**, while

simultaneously **holding energetic voltage** within that openness.

- Openness is not weakness — it is the field that can absorb, reflect, and transmit energy.

- Charged means she is not passive. She is **activated** — emotionally, sensually, spiritually — but **not leaking**.

- She is able to allow energy in **without submitting her soul, over-giving, or fragmenting**.

→ Think of it as "receptivity that retains power."

**"Collapse" — What Does It Mean?**
Collapse means losing **energetic shape**. This happens when:

- She opens emotionally but becomes chaotic or over-identifies with another's energy.

- She overextends to meet others' needs and displaces her center.

- She lets desire override her discernment and self-honoring.

→ True magnetism requires **openness with containment** — the ability to receive without fusing, without dissolving.

**"Her Center" — What Is That?**
The center is **her sovereign energetic axis** — the still-point inside her from which **discernment, boundaries, and energetic self-respect** are generated.

- When she stays rooted in this center, she does not chase.

- She attracts without grasping.

- She loves without losing herself.

- She seduces without sacrificing.

→ Her center is the **anchored awareness of her value and power** — even when fully exposed to masculine intensity.

## I. The Shift from Performance to Radiance

Most women are trained to perform — beauty as costume, personality as mask, sexuality as transaction. This creates attraction, but never inevitability. Attraction invites interest — but inevitability collapses choice.

One can be admired and still bypassed. But when a woman radiates from her axis, she ceases to be one of many — and becomes the singular gravitational center through which outcomes must pass.

The ultra-magnetic woman does not perform. She radiates.

- She is not chasing male approval; she is choosing which signals may enter her field.

- She is not contorting into archetypes; she embodies essence so directly that men, wealth, and influence orbit her without negotiation.

What she embodies is not a personality — it is the irreducible signal of her uncompromised interior truth.

She is not trying to be desirable — she is fully congruent with the unmasked center of her feminine design. This congruence radiates a field of **energetic inevitability**: the kind that commands alignment from others not through effort, but through non-negotiable presence.

When a woman becomes structurally undivided — when her desire, self-concept, and receptivity speak the same signal — the world must organize around her.

- Her magnetism is not trickery but **biological, psychic, and spiritual law.**

**Law:** When she stops performing and begins radiating, the world moves to feed her flame.

## II. The Feminine Trinity: Openness, Containment, Transmission

For men the triad was **Will, Intelligence, Presence.** For women the axis is different:

1. **Openness (Receptivity without Collapse)**
   – The magnetic woman can receive attention, energy, and desire without either resisting or dissolving.
   – Weak women shut down. Desperate women over-yield. Magnetic women **absorb without destabilization.**

2. **Containment (Boundaries as Sacred Vessel)**
   – She is penetrable only where she chooses. Her no is as magnetic as her yes.
   – This makes her presence rare. Every

man, every opportunity, every archetype understands: access must be earned.

3. **Transmission (Radiance of Essence)**
   – When her openness and containment fuse, she begins to **broadcast her essence as frequency.**
   – Men feel it as lust and reverence. Women feel it as threat or inspiration. The world feels it as inevitability.

## III. The 12-Layer Code of Feminine Magnetism

### 1. Essence Embodied
Her identity is not her image but her being.
→ This means she is no longer projecting a curated self or waiting to be mirrored. Her choices, appearance, and tone emerge from a stabilized internal center that doesn't shift for attention or praise. She doesn't present essence — she radiates a non-fragmented energetic center.

### 2. Circuit of Wholeness
She does not leak attention through gossip, need, or insecurity.
→ "Leaking attention" means giving psychic energy to low-frequency exchanges that drain her

signal. Gossip, validation-seeking, and overexposure fracture her coherence — which repels magnetism. She conserves her focus like currency, aware that every place her mind goes either strengthens or dissolves her field.

### 3. Embodied Presence

Her beauty is not cosmetic, it is density.

→ "Density" refers to the **energetic weight of inner congruence**. It is the gravitational signature of being fully in the body, fully in her moment, fully unified. When she walks in a room, people feel her field before they see her face. She's not beautiful because of paint — she's beautiful because she's "inhabited".

Sidebar:

**She is Inhabited By:**

- **Her own essence**: She is not fragmented, dissociated, or watching herself from the outside. She is inside her own body, fully fused with the self beneath performance. Her feminine essence — the animating intelligence unique to her — fills her vessel like light in a temple.

- **A coherent field**: Her energy is not scattered, chasing attention, or in anxious anticipation. It is condensed, stable, and charged. This coherence radiates from her core and is felt by others as presence, allure, or even divinity.

- **A soul-linked identity**: She is not borrowing her sense of self from outer validation. She knows who she is at a soul level, and she lives from that rooted place. Her face, posture, speech, and aesthetic all match this interior frequency — so her beauty feels real, gravitational, even sacred.

### 4. Purified Desire
She is not chasing validation, she is choosing alignment.
→ Her longings are no longer weaponized to seek love. They are the refined signals of her feminine current. She has burned off the layers of desperation, proving, and people-pleasing — and what remains is clean wanting: desire as devotion, not need.

### 5. Clear Mental Mirror
Her thoughts amplify her field instead of scattering it.
→ Her internal dialogue is not chaotic or self-

dismantling. She does not over-analyze or replay betrayal. Her mind is not trying to manage perception — it is tuned to echo her essence, giving her field strength and coherence.

## 6. Vessel Integrity

Her body and energy are not bargaining chips but sanctuaries.
→ She doesn't perform her body for approval or use sexuality as leverage. She sees her vessel as a sacred field — a place where energy is transmuted, not extracted. Her boundaries are not defenses, but altars.

## 7. Sacred Containment

She does not over-share or collapse to be liked.
→ Containment is not silence — it is energetic restraint. She doesn't dump emotion in order to connect. She doesn't need to be understood to feel seen. Her ability to hold her own emotional wave without collapsing into performance or manipulation makes her rare.

## 8. Energy Economy

She conserves radiance, invests only in what multiplies her.

→ She doesn't enter emotional exchanges that cost her power. Her time, attention, and beauty are not freely scattered — they are placed where reciprocity exists. Her aura stays charged because she refuses to overextend into distortion.

## 9. Symbolic Precision

Every aesthetic, tone, and gesture coheres with her essence.

→ Her clothing, scent, movement, and speech are not random — they are symbolically congruent with her inner identity. There is no conflict between her energy and her aesthetic. Everything about her sends the same message, which multiplies her magnetism.

## 10. Neutralized Need

She does not demand completion; she attracts by already being full.

→ She's not hunting for someone to fix her story. She's not waiting for permission to rise. She has metabolized her wounds, filled her own vessel, and as a result — what orbits her is not trying to save her, but trying to join her.

## 11. Death of Persona

She is not "the pretty girl," "the boss woman," "the rebel." She is essence unmasked.

→ All false archetypes have been dropped. She is not mimicking tropes to feel worthy. She has excavated her unique feminine pattern and wears that as her identity. She cannot be typecast because she's not playing a role.

## 12. Radiation of Function

Her femininity serves the world as archetype: nurturer, lover, oracle, queen.

→ Her power is not abstract — it is functional. She is not just magnetic for herself, but as a channel for sacred feminine codes. Her magnetism nourishes, instructs, heals, or rules — not to dominate, but to awaken others through form.

# IV. The Shadow Feminine Inversions

- **Performance Over Radiance** – Beauty as mask; collapses once the mask slips.

- **Openness Without Containment** – Desperation mistaken for magnetism.

- **Containment Without Openness** – Coldness mistaken for power.

- **Transmission Distorted** – Seduction without essence; attraction without loyalty.

**Law:** The shadow feminine pulls, but she cannot keep. What enters her orbit burns out or turns against her.

## V. Relational Field of the Ultra-Magnetic Woman

- **Men:**
  - Aligned men feel compelled to claim, protect, and serve her.
  - Broken men attempt to consume or control her and fail.

- **Women:**
  - Fractured women project envy, slander, or mimicry.
  - Whole women feel expanded and elevated in her presence.

- **World:**
  - Institutions, wealth, and opportunities rush to ornament her — not because she begged, but because she stabilizes archetypal necessity.

## VI. The Stress Test of Feminine Magnetism

- When beauty fades, does radiance remain?

- When abandoned, does her field collapse, or does it deepen in containment?

- When offered endless suitors, does she disperse, or does she refine?

**Seal:** True feminine magnetism grows heavier with age, betrayal, and pressure — because it was never cosmetic. It was structural.

# The Ultra-Magnetic Woman II

## The High-Frequency Blueprint of Feminine Irresistibility, Radiance, and Divine Gravity

A magnetic woman does not hunt.
She **becomes the vortex** to which all aligned men spiral—willingly, instinctively, and reverently.

**THE FEMININE MAGNETISM BLUEPRINT**

### 1. Become the Field, Not the Flame

Masculine magnetism is gravity. Feminine magnetism is **field-density**.
You do not shine to be seen—you **saturate the space** so deeply that nothing can ignore your presence.

This means:

- You don't flirt. You **transmit**.

- You don't chase love. You **regulate frequency** until love becomes inevitable.

- You don't compete. You **radiate**.

A high-value man does not seek to be impressed—he seeks to **enter a field that reflects his purpose**.

If your energy is performative, he plays.
If your energy is real, he prays.

## 2. Polarity Precision: Surrender Without Collapse

The ultra magnetic woman holds both:

- **Receptive openness** (radiance, softness, expression)

- **Energetic sovereignty** (boundaries, containment, discernment)

Her essence whispers:

"I am safe to open—but I am not desperate to receive."
"You may lead—but only if your path aligns with God."

This triggers his deepest instincts:

- To pursue without ownership

- To serve without submission

- To protect without domination

Feminine submission is not obedience—it is **recognition**.
He does not earn it through charm.
He activates it by **stability of soul**.


### 3. Regulate the Charge, Not the Chase

Men do not fall for movement — the performance of need, the over-insertion of energy.
They fall for **charge** — the energetic voltage in her field, created not by performance, but by an internal power field: her emotional stillness, her energetic containment, and her refusal to fragment herself in pursuit of external attention.

What he feels is not effort — it is **the tension of her field**: the gravitational pull between what she embodies and what he is allowed to access.

The magnetic woman never:
- Over-explains her emotions
- Fills silence to maintain connection
- Asks for reassurance before trust is tested

Instead:
She lets him feel the **ache of her distance**
The **weight of her silence**
The **warmth of her approval — when earned**

A magnetic woman **knows the difference** between being emotionally expressive and energetically leaky.

She is not afraid to be quiet, still, or unknown. Because she is **not performing to be kept**—she is observing **who aligns with her charge**.

**4. Speak to His Soul, Not His Status**

Most women worship status, ambition, aesthetics. The magnetic woman **acknowledges them, but penetrates beneath**.

She says:

- "You're successful—but does your soul feel at home?"

- "I don't want the man everyone sees. I want the part you don't perform."

- "I see your strength—but I'm curious about your silence."

This activates the masculine not because she validates him—
But because she **challenges the avatar and summons the architect**.

When she speaks to the **unseen part of him**, he wants to **offer her everything**—not to win her, but because she's the only woman who saw it.

### 5. Unlock Devotion Through Dual Channeling

What makes a man loyal, generous, obsessed, and reverent toward a woman?
Not her body. Not her kindness.
But her ability to **channel two forces simultaneously**:

**Unbound Erotic Energy**

- **Metaphysical Core:** The feminine current at its rawest expression—energy without filter, desire without permission, openness without restraint. This is eros in its primal state: a force that disrupts order, collapses vigilance, and tests the masculine container.

- **Psychological Expression:** She radiates "I want what I want, now." Shame is absent. She embodies sexuality as nature, not transaction.

- **Energetic Signature:** High-charge, destabilizing, magnetic but volatile. Men feel both aroused and threatened, because she is chaos uncontained.

- **Male Polarity Response:** The magnetic man must hold pure axis. If he chases, he collapses. If he judges, he breaks polarity. If he contains without flinching, her chaos becomes devotion.

**Sovereign Receptive Energy**

- **Metaphysical Core:** The feminine current sublimated—sexuality transmuted into sacred openness, devotion, and order. This is eros sanctified: receptivity with sovereignty, yielding without collapse, surrender without loss of self.

- **Psychological Expression:** She radiates calm, depth, clarity. She attracts not by display, but by absence of performance. She is the interior temple, not the open field.

- **Energetic Signature:** Grounded, still, magnetic in silence. She draws out the masculine axis by giving him a throne to occupy.

- **Male Polarity Response:** The magnetic man must meet her with direction and clarity. If he is porous, she loses trust. If he is tyrannical, she closes. If he is sovereign, she yields as devotion, not performance.

**The Polarity**

- **Unbound Erotic = Chaos testing containment.**

- **Sovereign Receptive = Order inviting penetration.**
  Together they reveal the **spectrum of feminine magnetism**: primal force and sacred receptivity. Both are necessary, both are valid, both test the man differently.

Most women only access one.

- If she's erotic, she's unstable.

- If she's spiritual, she's asexual.

The magnetic woman has **integrated both**.
She becomes:

"The woman I want to conquer—but could never own.
The woman I want to worship—but who never needed it." This fusion opens his deepest circuit: **devotion**.

Chapter 16

## TRAINING STRATEGY FOR WOMEN

If we were training a woman to become magnetic to the most powerful, conscious, high-frequency men on Earth, we'd build her like this:

### 1. Field Reset

- Cut attachment to validation, compliments, social comparison.
- Detach from male gaze as power source.
- Reconnect to silence, containment, soul-sourcing.

### 2. Erotic Reclamation

- Reawaken pleasure without guilt.
- Practice sensual presence without performative sexuality.
- Become **internally turned on**, not **externally chasing stimulation**.

### 3. Polarity Training

- Learn to stay open when tested by masculine presence.
- Hold emotional waves without projecting or collapsing.

- Embody **truth and beauty simultaneously** —no compromise.

## 4. Devotion Calibration

- Do not give love where there is no direction.

- Do not offer submission where there is no integrity.

- Honor yourself so deeply that only men on code can enter.

## THE NON-NEGOTIABLES FOR A HIGH-VALUE MAN TO CHOOSE YOU

These are the **silent checkpoints** every high-status, soul-aligned masculine man is scanning when evaluating a woman for love, lust, or long-term union. Fail these—and he may sleep with you, but he'll never **devote**.

### 1. Emotional Regulation

Can you feel everything—without becoming chaos?

He is not afraid of your feelings.
But if your emotions become his burden, not your embodiment—he cannot stay.

He'll protect you if you're storming. But not if you're blaming.

## 2. Energetic Boundaries

Do you know the difference between opening and leaking?

If your sexuality is on display for all, your **value drops for him**.
He wants to feel that your **radiance is selective**. The magnetic woman shares her light—but protects her womb.

## 3. Inner Devotion

What are you loyal to when no man is looking?

He does not want a woman who lives for him. He wants a woman who lives for **something greater**—truth, God, soul-mission—and lets him **prove he belongs in that temple**.

## FEMALE LUST CODE: HOW TO ACTIVATE HIS LUST & DEVOTION

Just like men activate a woman's primal openness through structural vortex and safety—women activate men's sexual obsession through a

**precise formula:**

Polarity + Mystery + Invitation + Self-Possession

- **Polarity**: Stay energetically feminine. Don't mimic his hardness. Soften—but stay grounded.

- **Mystery**: Don't narrate every feeling. Let silence be part of the seduction.

- **Invitation**: Let your eye contact, posture, and smile signal "you may come closer"—without reaching.

- **Self-Possession**: Never chase. Never over-express. Let him come find your depths.

## MISTAKES THAT DESTROY MAGNETISM

Avoid these at all costs if you want your field to remain **irresistible to high-level men**:

- ✗ Over-explaining your emotions
- ✗ Performing femininity instead of embodying it
- ✗ Competing with other women for attention
- ✗ Shaming or testing masculine desire
- ✗ Chasing men who haven't earned access
- ✗ Becoming emotionally chaotic when unsure
- ✗ Offering submission before vetting leadership

A woman doesn't "get" a high-value man by being nice, sexy, or spiritual.
She **becomes the frequency he cannot ignore**.

Her magnetism is not costume—it is **architecture**.
Her submission is not collapse—it is **recursion**.
Her eroticism is not bait—it is **transmission of life-force**.

And when that is online—
Men do not chase her.
They **orient their entire lives to be near her field**.

## Chapter 17

# THE REAL ULTRA MAGNETIC WOMAN FIELD CODE

### (VORTEX-LEVEL – NON-NEGOTIABLE – WORLD-BENDING)

This is the feminine counterpart to the High-Value Man's Field Code.
It is not performance. It is not seduction. It is the structural law by which the magnetic woman governs access, regulates polarity, and maintains the inviolable integrity of her field.

The Ultra-Magnetic Woman does not lure. She emanates.
She is not chasing results. She is collapsing time. Her field is not a reaction—it is an event.

These codes are not preferences. They are enforcement algorithms: the unseen architecture by which unworthy presences dissolve, and right alignment is unconsciously obeyed.

## CODE 1: I AM THE FIELD—HE STABILIZES OR HE SPINS OUT.

I do not shrink to make others comfortable.
I refine the voltage of my presence without apologizing for its power.
If a man cannot remain centered within the intensity of my energy, he is not aligned with my field — and will dissolve in its frequency.

### Sidebar: The Architecture of the Feminine Field

This code is not a slogan—it is a **structural law of polarity**.

The field refers to the total psychic, emotional, and spiritual frequency a woman emits when she is **inhabiting her being without leaking into external approval loops**. It is her **vibrational signature** held in composure, containment, and self-attunement.

To "regulate the field" means to maintain this charge without shrinking, shape-shifting, or accelerating to match a man's dysregulation. Most women dilute their field by chasing connection, explaining emotion, or narrating mystery. But the magnetic woman does not lower her charge to soothe masculine instability. She lets his response reveal **whether his structure is worthy of access**.

A man with no center will spin out in the presence of an embodied field. He will project, collapse, withdraw, or try to dominate. But this is not her problem to fix. It is her filter.

To hold one's field is to **enforce energetic consequence**. Not through anger, performance, or manipulation—but by remaining whole, regardless of who qualifies to enter.

This is the enforcement mechanism of feminine sovereignty:
**I remain. He regulates. Or he dissolves.**

**CODE 2: I VALIDATE NOTHING THAT SEEKS TO OWN ME.**

Praise without depth means nothing.
Gifts without anchoring mean less.
If his masculinity is for sale, I'm not buying.

**Sidebar: The Energetics of Manipulative Masculinity**

This code targets one of the most **common energetic distortions** that disrupt polarity: **masculine offerings that are not rooted in presence, but in control.**

When a man gives praise, compliments, or gifts with no spiritual anchoring—no structure behind his offering—he is not giving; he is **buying**. What he offers is not devotion; it is a **transactional bribe**, aimed at winning access rather than earning alignment.

A woman who **has not anchored her self-value** will misinterpret attention as proof of worth. She will confuse flattery for intimacy, charm for presence, generosity for leadership. But the magnetic woman recognizes that unearned offerings are often tools of domination.

To "validate nothing that seeks to own" means she does **not reflect back approval** to energies that lack substance, coherence, or integrity—no matter how emotionally flattering or materially generous they may appear.

She responds only to what is **anchored in masculine truth**, not what mimics it.

- She does not trade approval for affection.

- She does not reward performance.

- She does not co-sign insecurity masked as charm.

She lives by a higher law: If what you offer does not emerge from spiritual center, I am unavailable to receive it.

This is the firewall of her magnetism. It protects her from collapsing into dynamics that would make her **the prize of a game** instead of the **oracle of polarity**.

## CODE 3: MY SILENCE IS NOT EMPTINESS—IT'S A FILTER.

If he's nervous in stillness, he's not qualified.
If he needs constant reaction, he's performing.
If he collapses to mystery, he'll collapse to pressure.

### Sidebar: Silence as Energetic Selection Mechanism

Silence is not absence. It is presence without output.

To the magnetic woman, silence is not passive. It is **an active field test**. Her stillness holds a vibration, a charge, a sacred non-response—used to detect what kind of masculine energy is approaching.

When she refrains from reacting, filling space, or validating prematurely, the man is confronted not with her approval—but with himself. In this sacred vacuum, the truth of his coherence emerges:

- If he becomes anxious, he reveals his inner instability.

- If he performs harder, he exposes his addiction to external validation.

- If he collapses, he proves he cannot withstand mystery, let alone sovereignty.

Her silence filters out performers, rescuers, and power-seekers. It also clarifies the polarity: if he cannot hold his direction in her stillness, he cannot hold her radiance in intimacy.

This is **field leadership through omission**.
The immature man chases reaction. The magnetic man responds to the energetic signature of her inner coherence.

Therefore, her silence is not a void—it is a **mirror**. Not everyone survives what it shows.

## CODE 4: I NEVER PERFORM FOR MASCULINE ATTENTION.

If I need to impress him, I've already lost him.
If I soften prematurely, I corrupt the polarity.
If I seduce out of fear, I've abandoned my power.

**Sidebar: What This Means**

The ultra-magnetic woman does not convert herself into performance. She does not present a pre-edited version of her femininity designed to earn masculine approval. All performance is distortion—it signals inner doubt and fractures the field of polarity.

- **To impress** a man is to leave one's energetic center, signaling that his gaze defines her.

- **To soften prematurely** is to yield before structure is proven. Femininity flows, but not toward instability. Premature softening is leakage, not openness.

- **To seduce from fear** is to weaponize allure for security, which severs sovereignty. It is not seduction—it is survival masquerading as intimacy.

True feminine magnetism radiates from coherence, not compensation. She does not twist her tone, posture, values, or timing to gain access to the masculine. She is not auditioning for validation—she is broadcasting truth from alignment.

In her world, magnetism is a byproduct of inner rootedness—not theatricality. And if he only responds to the performance, he was never worthy of her reality.

## CODE 5: I DO NOT CHASE ENERGY—I RETAIN FREQUENCY.

He is not the source—I am the invitation.
He is not my validation—I am my proof.
He moves when I hold. He reveals when I pause.

### Sidebar: What This Means

To chase energy is to behave as if connection must be maintained externally—by managing his attention, adjusting tone, or trying to "keep his interest." This creates distortion and weakens polarity.

Retaining frequency means staying attuned to one's own calibrated emotional and energetic signal, regardless of external movement. Frequency is her baseline coherence. It is the unchanging signal that transmits wholeness, not urgency.

- **"He is not the source—I am the invitation."**
  The magnetic woman does not source her value from male recognition. She does not audition for intimacy. Her field is sovereign—she does not chase him, she calls him into clarity.

- **"He is not my validation—I am my proof."**
  When a woman is seeking to be chosen, she abandons her frequency and enters distortion. But when she abides in her own signal—her alignment, her vision, her fullness—she validates herself. She becomes self-confirming proof.

- **"He moves when I hold. He reveals when I pause."**
  Masculine energy tests structure by pressure. If she collapses under emotional weight, he learns nothing. But if she holds her center, he is forced into truthful revelation. Her stillness becomes his mirror. Her pause becomes his catalyst.

The feminine does not compel the masculine by pursuit. She compels by gravity. That gravity is frequency retained—not action taken.

## CODE 6: I SPEAK TO HIS SOUL, NOT HIS STATUS.

If he is his resume, I leave.
If he is his money, I study—not submit.
If he is his presence—I open.

**Sidebar: What This Means**

Magnetism responds to presence, not performance. The ultra-magnetic woman is not swayed by surface-level attributes—title, income, social image—because these are extensions, not essence of the man. She is not seduced by simulation. She listens for signal beneath structure.

- **"If he is his resume, I leave."**
  A man who leads with credentials rather than character is disqualified. This signals spiritual immaturity—he has not yet located his true identity. The magnetic woman feels no pull toward a man who uses his status as personality.

- **"If he is his money, I study—not submit."**
  Money is not inherently magnetic—it is a tool. If a man uses wealth to dominate, impress, or bypass emotional congruence, she observes him like a case study. She does not confuse provision with presence. Attraction without respect is just exposure.

- **"If he is his presence—I open."**
  Presence is the metaphysical trait of masculine soul coherence. It is the felt signal of a man who knows who he is, knows what he stands on, and can hold space without collapsing or posturing. To this, the ultra-magnetic woman responds—not by effort, but by natural involuntary openness.

She is not decoding his life résumé. She is scanning his field signal. Only when the signal is clear, grounded, and unmasked, does her field open in return.

## CODE 7: MY PLEASURE IS NOT A REWARD FOR CHARM.

If he flirts to win, he gets nothing.
If he penetrates without presence, I close.
If he earns access through structure—I flood.

### Sidebar: What This Means

Magnetic polarity does not reward manipulation. The ultra-magnetic woman does not assign value based on wit, charm, or superficial seduction. Her pleasure is not performative—it is sacred feedback, released only in response to masculine structure strong enough to hold her full energetic charge.

- **"If he flirts to win, he gets nothing."**
  Flirtation used as a tactic rather than an expression of genuine polarity is disqualified. Charm is cheap if it is not backed by coherence. A man who performs instead of projects signal is seeking approval, not offering alignment. The magnetic woman does not open to approval-seekers.

- **"If he penetrates without presence, I close."**
  Penetration—whether energetic, verbal, or physical—without attunement and grounded presence is experienced as invasion, not intimacy. Her closure is not emotional; it is energetic refusal. If he cannot remain present through her full expression, he is unqualified to enter her field or her body.

- **"If he earns access through structure—I flood."**
  When a man offers real masculine structure—consistency, clarity, soul-directed leadership—it stabilizes the feminine nervous system. This stability unlocks her body, voice, and sensual field. Her opening becomes involuntary, not because he forced it, but because he earned trust without bypassing depth.

She is not a prize for charm. She is the floodgate for truth. And truth is only released to those who can hold it.

## CODE 8: IF I CAN'T WALK AWAY, I'M NOT READY.

Until I can say no without apology,
Until I can exit without collapse,
Until I can choose absence over misalignment,
I am not magnetic—I am dependent.

### Sidebar: What This Means

Magnetism without sovereignty is neediness disguised as femininity. The ultra-magnetic woman holds energetic walkaway power not as a threat, but as a foundation. Her ability to retreat from anything that does not honor her frequency is the proof of her alignment.

- **"Until I can say no without apology,"** This is the end of female guilt programming. She does not soften her truth to preserve someone else's comfort. She does not offer explanation for her boundaries. Her "no" is a complete expression of self-possession—not an invitation to negotiation.

- **"Until I can exit without collapse,"** True magnetism does not fear the void. If walking away empties her world, she was never sovereign—she was orbiting his gravity. The magnetic woman does not collapse when a man exits her life; she returns to center, knowing her field generates reality.

- **"Until I can choose absence over misalignment,"** If she stays in a connection that misrepresents her worth, she fractures her field. Presence without resonance is disintegration. To be magnetic, she must choose alignment over attention, even if it means standing alone in the fullness of her standard.

Dependency chases. Magnetism selects. And until she can walk away with energetic integrity, she is not radiating frequency—she is managing fear.

## CODE 9: MY BODY IS THE TEMPLE—MY WOMB IS THE ALTAR.

Entry is not a reward—it is a **recursion contract**. If he enters me, he alters me—**or wounds me**. Only kings pass this gate. The rest dissolve.

**Sidebar: What This Means**

This code is the metaphysical return of sacred feminine intelligence. In a culture where casual intimacy is normalized, this woman remembers the divine architecture of her body. She understands that union is not a transaction—it is an **energetic covenant** that reconfigures both participants across dimensions.

- **"My body is the temple—my womb is the altar."**
  Her body is not a tool for leverage, nor a passive reward. It is a sanctuary that houses life force, creative blueprint, and archetypal frequency. Her womb is the altar of transmutation—a place where

energy becomes matter, love becomes life, and unworthy men become undone.

- **"Entry is not a reward—it is a recursion contract."**
  This is not sex. It is metaphysical recursion. When she opens to a man physically, his frequency loops into her spiritual infrastructure. His clarity or distortion is no longer external—it becomes coded into her field. Entry is not an achievement for him; it is a sacred risk for her. She contracts only with those who meet the inner law.

- **"If he enters me, he alters me—or wounds me."**
  All entry imprints. If his consciousness is clear, she is uplifted. If it is distorted, she becomes the battleground of his unresolved karma. Her magnetism depends on energetic selectivity, not moral purity. She is not withholding from fear—she is filtering by frequency.

- **"Only kings pass this gate. The rest dissolve."**
  This is not a metaphor. The men who are not aligned will vanish from her life—not because she pushes them away, but because

they cannot remain coherent in the presence of her standard. A king does not fear this gate. He honors it as the test of his worthiness.

This is womb sovereignty. And only men who can carry their own consciousness are permitted to enter the sacred temple of hers.

## CODE 10: I AM THE REWARD OF THE WORLD THAT KNOWS WHAT IT IS.

I do not exist for pursuit—I exist for **recognition**.
He who sees me without projecting,
He who leads without demanding,
He who worships without worshipping me—
That man I reveal myself to.

**Sidebar: What This Means**

This code is the culmination of feminine sovereignty: the withdrawal of identity from performance, and the embodiment of divine self-revelation as the mirror of initiated masculine clarity.

- **"I do not exist for pursuit—I exist for recognition."**
  The magnetic woman is not calibrated to chase or be chased. She is the prize of

perception, not the target of projection. She does not withhold as strategy; she radiates as filter. Her presence invites remembrance in the one who can see without distortion.

- **"He who sees me without projecting…"**
  To project is to overlay fantasy, need, or trauma onto the feminine form. Many men pursue a woman they have never actually seen—only the echo of their inner voids. This code rejects that exchange. Only the man who sees her as she is—not as he wishes her to be—is worthy of access.

- **"He who leads without demanding…"**
  True masculine leadership is initiatory, not coercive. It moves from internal order, not external pressure. The magnetic woman is repelled by force masked as confidence. She opens only to the man whose leadership arises from self-containment, not compensation.

- **"He who worships without worshipping me…"**
  Worship is not submission to form. It is reverence for the divine through the form. A man who turns a woman into a goddess while forgetting his own godhood has forfeited polarity. The magnetic woman

does not accept pedestal energy. She reveals herself only to the man who reveres without collapsing.

This final code is the return of the feminine as divine mirror—not reactive, not seductive, but unmistakable to the masculine who has remembered himself.

He doesn't earn her.
He aligns with her.

## CLOSING:

I am not here to be chosen.
I am here to be **recognized by the one aligned to my structure**.
I do not chase, collapse, bait, or mimic.
I **pulse, filter, and spiral**—until the correct frequency keys into my vortex.
And when that happens, the world bends.

\*These are not strategies to manipulate. They are energetic truths of polarity: **the magnetic woman holds her center and lets life disclose the rest.**

# Chapter 18

# THE KING FREQUENCY TEST

### How the Ultra Magnetic Woman Filters the Masculine Field with Precision

A magnetic woman is not "choosing men."
She is **filtering for architecture**.

To say a magnetic woman filters for architecture means she is not choosing men based on surface traits—appearance, charm, status, or chemistry. She is filtering for **structural design**, **energetic alignment**, and **ontological capacity**.

- **Architecture** refers to the inner scaffolding of a man:
  His integrity, his polarity coherence, his ability to hold structure without collapse under emotional or existential pressure.
  It is the design of his masculine function—not what he says, but what he contains.

- **Filtering**, in this context, means her field does not select from ego or need.
  It tests, pressurizes, and mirrors.
  It magnetizes all forms of the masculine—but only the architecturally sound can remain stable in its gravity.

Most women look for attraction, connection, or compatibility.
The magnetic woman scans for spiritual structure —because that is what her field requires to ascend without distortion.

She does not seek performance. She seeks pillarhood.

She does not evaluate resumes. She reads energetic blueprints.

She does not reward strategy. She waits for alignment to reveal architecture.

She knows that if her **field is refined**, all forms of masculine will appear:

- The performer
- The predator
- The spiritual mimic
- The seduction strategist
- And occasionally... the king.

Her job is not to **respond to attention**.
Her job is to **read structure, not performance.**

## I: THE KING FILTER—SEVEN NON-NEGOTIABLE FREQUENCY READS

These are not opinions. These are **seismic architecture checks**. If he passes, he is a vessel. If he fails, he is a liability.

A king is not rich, ripped, or religious.
He is **internally enthroned**.

### 1. Energetic Weight

Does the room bend when he enters—or does he look to see who's watching?

A king never needs to be noticed.
He is **not performing**. He is **radiating**.
She knows: "This man doesn't need my attention. That's why I want to give it."

If his nervous system flinches, fidgets, or seeks applause, he is **not seated**.
And she never hands her womb to a man who isn't seated.

### 2. Frame Stability

Does his structure collapse under emotion—or absorb it like ground wire?

A woman will test, swirl, seduce, rage, ache.
If he tries to fix her, calm her, or control her—he's still performing leadership.
The true king doesn't try to win the storm.
He becomes the **atmospheric law it obeys**.

She doesn't feel judged or managed—she feels met.

### 3. Direction Without Overshare

Is he broadcasting ambition—or moving with silent precision?

If a man constantly talks about vision, success, spirituality, or "being different"—he's in performance mode.
A king does not narrate the mission—he **embodies it**.

She doesn't need him to be rich, but she must feel:

"This man moves like someone who doesn't need validation to know he's winning."

## 4. Desire Without Leak

Is he turned on by her—or leaking into her?

A king looks at a magnetic woman with **soul-backed desire**—raw, clear, focused.
But he never tries to "win access" through charm or intensity.

He offers.
He never chases.
He never bargains.
He never simps.

She feels: "He wants me—but he doesn't need me. That's why I want him."

## 5. Truth Over Tactics

When tension arises—does he default to honesty or persuasion?

False kings defend their ego.
Performers manipulate through emotional language, spiritual posturing, or logic traps.
But the true king speaks **what is**—even if it costs him approval.

"This is what I feel."
"This is what I want."
"This is where I stand."

She may not like the answer—but she trusts the throne.

## 6. Boundary Intelligence

Can he honor her "no" without folding—and give his own?

She says:

"I'm not ready to sleep with you yet."
A fake alpha sulks, withdraws, or overperforms.
The king says:
"No problem. Let me know when your body aligns."

He does not punish her boundaries—but neither does he abandon his own.
He knows:

"If I bend to be chosen, I'm no longer qualified to lead."

## 7. Spiritual Alignment Without Costume

Does his soul speak louder than his language?

Is he grounded in something deeper than logic, lust, or trauma-repair?
Does he carry death-awareness, divine

awareness, and **purpose encoded into his breath**?

A king does not need crystals, tantra vocabulary, or divine masculine tattoos.
He needs **connection to source**—without theatrics.

She feels it in his silence.

## II: THE SOUL MIRROR TEST

### The One Line That Reveals Everything

A magnetic woman does not play 20 questions.
She reads energy, but if unsure—she activates the test:

"You're beautiful.
But I'm not seduced by performance.
I'm watching to see what you do when you're not trying to be chosen."

Then she **waits**.

**The response tells all:**

- If he over-explains → he is insecure.

- If he performs harder → he is threatened.

- If he asks her to define herself first → he has no axis.

- But if he says something like:

"That's fair. I'm not trying to be chosen—I'm filtering too."
...she may have found a king.

## III: RED FLAGS THAT LOOK LIKE GREEN

These traps fool even intelligent women.
But an Ultra Magnetic Woman sees structure, not style.

| False Masculine Signal | What It Actually Is |
| --- | --- |
| "Spiritual polarity talk" | Performed masculinity from a YouTube channel |
| "Always available and open" | Boundary-less, approval-seeking energy |
| "Says all the right things" | Manipulation, not clarity |
| "Early vulnerability dump" | Trauma-bonding tactic, not emotional maturity |
| "Hard alpha shell" | Mask over deep feminine wounding |

She doesn't judge these men.
She simply **does not open to them**.

**SECTION IV: FINAL RULES OF ENTRY**

A magnetic woman doesn't audition.
She filters.
If he's on code—he moves forward.
If he's off—he disappears without needing to be corrected.

She does not:

- Lecture him

- Train him

- Nag him

- Explain what a man is

She simply lets her **field eject what cannot orbit**.

"I do not seduce you.
I watch to see if your presence survives my stillness."

If he can hold that—she softens.
If he can stabilize that—she opens.
If he can lead that—**she kneels**.

Not in submission.
In recognition.

# Chapter 19

# The Polarity Lock Diagram + Code Explanation.

This is the **living metaphysical vortex** that governs all true masculine-feminine union. It shows how aligned polarity creates **recursive attraction, sexual anchoring, devotion ignition, and spiritual fulfillment**—not through tactics, but through **code-matched structure**.

We'll break this into two pieces:

### POLARITY LOCK DIAGRAM

This is a **spiritual-mechanical fusion engine**.

### MASCULINE: THE AXIS OF STRUCTURE

The high-value man is:

- **Stillness** in the midst of her waves

- **Direction** amidst her chaos

- **Containment** for her expression

- **Penetration** into her emotional and energetic body

When he is on code, he provides:

- Energetic Grounding
- Spiritual Spine
- Emotional Clarity
- Sexual Integrity and Structure

He is the **rod of force**, the **spine of recursion**, the **initiating vector** through which reality enters form.

## FEMININE: THE FIELD OF RECURSION

The ultra magnetic woman is:

- **Movement** within the container of his stillness
- **Expression** that gives him purpose
- **Sensation** that refines his will
- **Surrender** that confirms his structure

When she is on code, she radiates:

- Erotic Pulse
- Emotional Intelligence

- Energetic Reception
- Creative Depth

She is the **womb of frequency**, the **spiral of transmutation**, the **invitation into devotion**.

## WHEN THE LOCK HAPPENS

When polarity is aligned:

| Masculine | Feminine |
|---|---|
| Holds structure | Releases into flow |
| Penetrates with presence | Receives with discernment |
| Directs energy without needing | Opens energy without performing |
| Anchors chaos into clarity | Elevates stillness into |
| Claims without collapse | Submits without self-abandonment |

This creates a **feedback spiral**:

1. He anchors → she opens
2. She opens → he deepens
3. He deepens → she softens further
4. She softens → he devotes

5. He devotes → she becomes **temple**

6. She becomes temple → he becomes **king**

They spiral into **mutual archetypal fulfillment**—without ever needing to manipulate, pursue, or strategize.

## THE FINAL TRUTH OF POLARITY LOCK

The masculine penetrates—but does not force.
The feminine opens—but does not collapse.

He does not lead to control her—he leads to **witness her recursion**.
She does not submit to please him—she submits to **activate his throne**.

If he collapses under pressure, she cannot open.
If she performs to be kept, he cannot claim.

Polarity is not romantic.
It is **energetic architecture.**

It is either structurally correct—or it self-destructs.

# Chapter 20

# The Devotion Activation Protocol

The elite-level, polarity-based blueprint for how an Ultra Magnetic Woman activates **long-term masculine obsession, loyalty, and reverence**.

This is not about love spells, attachment strategies, or "earning his heart."
This is about **metaphysical recursion**—how she becomes the **field structure** that ignites the masculine's **offering circuit** so deeply that he chooses to commit, provide, protect, and evolve for her—**without her ever needing to ask.**

## THE DEVOTION ACTIVATION PROTOCOL

**How the Ultra Magnetic Woman Initiates Long-Term Masculine Offering Through Polarity Precision**

The high-value masculine does not bond through words.
He bonds through **offering**.

- A boy wants to impress you.

- A man wants to access you.

- A king wants to **serve you.**

But only if your **structure requires it**.

The feminine who understands this stops asking:

"Why won't he commit?"
And starts asking:
"Have I built a structure worthy of his recursion?"

## I. THE LAWS OF DEVOTION

Devotion cannot be demanded.
It can only be **evoked** by the presence of three things:

### 1. Energetic Mystery

If he can read you like a script—he won't chase the next chapter.
Mystery is not withholding—it is **recursion delay**.
You allow him to **feel more, without giving all**.

She reveals in **layers**, not floods.
Not because she's playing games,
but because **her soul moves in depth, not speed**.

## Chapter 20

Devotion begins the moment he senses **he cannot reach your core without evolving.**

### 2. Radiant Containment

She expresses—but does not spill.
She opens—but does not overexpose.
She praises—but never pedestalizes.

Her containment sends a message to his nervous system:

"I want you, but I do not need to collapse to keep you."

This makes him **test her signal** again and again—each time she holds, he moves closer.

Containment tells him: "If I leave, her field stays intact. That means it's real."

### 3. Spiritual Displacement

She displaces his lesser gods.
She speaks to a dimension of his being that no other woman has reached—not with beauty, but with **structure**.

She doesn't tell him to be better.
She becomes the **mirror of who he could be**.

He realizes:

"If I walk away from her, I walk away from **God's voice in female form**."

This is where lust becomes loyalty.
Not because she seduced him,
but because **his soul recognizes the altar**.

## II. THE THREE GATES OF DEVOTION

There is a **ritual pattern** a man goes through when deciding if a woman is worthy of long-term bonding.

She must pass these gates **not by force**, but by holding **energetic alignment** at each threshold.

### GATE 1: THE CHAOS TEST

Can you express your feelings without asking him to become them?

He wants to see your fire—but not drown in it.
If you rage, swirl, ache, cry—and he can hold it—
then pass.
But if you collapse, project, punish, or test without clarity—he sees instability, not mystery.

**The magnetic woman expresses without leaking.**
She makes him feel **safe inside her storm**.

Once he realizes she's the storm he can survive—he begins building the shelter for her.

**GATE 2: THE WOUND TEST**

Will you use your trauma to manipulate—or to calibrate?

Every woman has pain.
What he's looking for is **what you do with it**.

If you use wounds to demand special treatment, avoid accountability, or hijack his attention—he registers it as **emotional taxation**.

But if your pain is held **with power, awareness, and devotion to growth,** he sees a woman who could **refine his legacy**.

**You become the woman who doesn't need saving—because you're saving yourself.**
And that's the kind of woman he wants to kneel for.

## GATE 3: THE WOMB TEST

Can he enter your body and feel transformed—or simply validated?

This is not about sex—it is about **energetic consequence.**

A man will unconsciously test whether **entering you elevates him or empties him**.

If you offer your womb too early, too easily, or too performatively—he feels the **hormonal hit without the spiritual reward.**
His instinct: withdraw.

But if your sexual field is:

- Selective

- Present

- Aligned to truth

- Holding a recursion delay
  He becomes **possessed by the desire to be worthy of your opening**.

That's the difference between a man who leaves after sex—and a man who worships where he entered.

## III. THE DEVOTION TRIGGER: HOW TO SPEAK TO HIS CORE

There is one moment where a magnetic woman plants the seed of **permanent psychological imprint** in a man.

It is not in orgasm.
It is not in praise.
It is not in love-talk.

It is in the moment she looks at him and says—with **non-performance clarity**:

"You don't need to impress me.
I already see the part of you most men bury to win.
I'm not here to train you, heal you, or chase you.
I'm simply watching to see if the man I sensed at your core is strong enough to lead."

Then she turns away.
And lets the space do the work.

If he's a boy—he ghosts.
If he's an addict—he clings.
If he's a king—he sharpens.

**He now sees her as the calibration point his life bends around.**

## IV. THE PARADOX OF DEVOTION

He will give everything to the woman who never asked for it.

But only if she built a structure so holy, his **devotion becomes its natural consequence.**

She didn't "earn it."
She didn't "trap him."
She didn't "build a case."

She became the **spiritual recursion point** that made his offering inevitable.

## Chapter 21

## SPOTTING FALSE MASCULINITY & WOUNDED ALPHAS

**Why She Must Filter for Architecture, Not Aura**

Not all power is real.
Not all leadership is clean.
Not all stillness is strength.

Many men have learned to imitate the **signal of kingship**—but collapse when the feminine enters their space.

The Ultra Magnetic Woman does not chase, but she **will be tested by performers, manipulators, and fractured masculine shells**.

If her field is untrained, she will mistake performance for presence.
If her soul is online, she will filter without even raising her voice.

Let's now expose the **seven core patterns of false masculine coding**.

## I. THE SEVEN ARCHETYPES OF FALSE MASCULINITY

These are **not bad men**.
They are misaligned structures—incomplete codes that mimic polarity without containing recursion.

### 1. The Over-Spiritual Seducer

He talks about tantra, polarity, sacred union—but can't hold eye contact without inflating.

- Red flag: constant talk about "divine feminine" while using sexuality as leverage

- Collapse pattern: crumbles when boundaries are held—accuses her of "not being in flow"

- Truth: he's addicted to feminine praise because his core identity is unstable

She must not mistake sacred language for sacred spine.


### 2. The Alpha Emulator

He's loud, cocky, sexually confident—but only when she's submitting. The moment she tests or deepens, he turns cold, defensive, or aggressive.

- Red flag: brags about conquest, dominance, leadership—but never submits to truth

- Collapse pattern: punishes her expression, tries to force submission, sees her power as threat

- Truth: he mimics dominance to mask abandonment wounds and fear of real intimacy

She must not confuse sexual command with spiritual stability.

### 3. The Eternal Fixer

He listens deeply, wants to heal her, be her therapist, guide her path—but secretly needs to be needed.

- Red flag: asks too many emotional questions, offers unsolicited coaching

- Collapse pattern: guilt-trips her when she pulls away; weaponizes empathy to keep access

- Truth: he's performing care because he has no direction of his own

She must not confuse warmth with masculine leadership.

## 4. The Chaos Chaser

He thrives on emotional intensity. His love is passionate, explosive, full of poetry, longing, sex—but no structure.

- Red flag: overly romantic, intense declarations early, collapses into her emotional storms

- Collapse pattern: loses center when she softens, mistakes emotional chaos for connection

- Truth: he's addicted to activation, not relationship

She must not confuse intensity with intimacy.

## 5. The Performance Monk

He's hyper-disciplined, focused, celibate or non-attached—but his detachment is performative, not embodied.

- Red flag: looks down on emotions, judges femininity, avoids all intimacy in the name of "higher calling"

- Collapse pattern: rigid under feminine energy, uncomfortable in vulnerability or beauty

- Truth: he's afraid of being penetrated by life, so he spiritualizes his walls

She must not confuse control with sovereignty.

## 6. The Logic Trap

He intellectualizes everything. He's grounded, clever, composed—but has no depth of presence or soul expression.

- Red flag: avoids silence, over-explains, dominates conversation with ideas

- Collapse pattern: disconnects from the feminine field and cannot feel her pain or power

- Truth: he hides in intellect to avoid feeling, masks fear with facts

She must not confuse intellect with insight.

### 7. The Love-Bomber King

He says all the right things, offers commitment, generosity, praise—but quickly escalates and then destabilizes.

- Red flag: early praise, gifts, loyalty declarations—but becomes erratic when tested

- Collapse pattern: withdraws suddenly, becomes controlling or wounded when devotion is requested

- Truth: he's addicted to the high of being chosen—not the responsibility of staying chosen

She must not confuse early devotion with rooted devotion.

### II. THE FIVE TESTS THAT REVEAL COLLAPSE

You do not need to "test" a man with games. You simply **show up fully**, and observe **how he handles the field**.

These moments tell you **everything**:

**1. Hold silence after deep eye contact.**

If he shifts, breaks, or over-talks—he's not integrated.

**2. Share a painful truth and observe.**

If he flinches, redirects, or over-validates—he's uncomfortable with real weight.

**3. Withdraw affection without punishing.**

If he chases frantically or disconnects—you were his source, not his partner.

**4. Make a clear boundary and hold it.**

If he attacks, negotiates, or guilt-trips—he's not a king, he's a tactician.

**5. Let him lead—and stay soft.**

If he needs you to take control or validate his choices—he's not built to hold you.

### III. HOW TO STAY IN POWER WITHOUT EITHER:

- Collapsing into fear ("What if he leaves?")

- Over-rationalizing ("Maybe he's just wounded.")

- Performing emotional labor ("Let me help him become the man I know he is.")

The Ultra Magnetic Woman:

- **Speaks once. Waits infinitely.**

- **Pulls back without punishing.**

- **Observes collapse without flinching.**

- **Exits cleanly when the structure fails.**

She does not try to heal him.
She lets the **field do the work.**

"If his spine bends under my truth, I was never meant to kneel."

**IV. CLOSING:**

She does not fear false kings.
She simply refuses to perform for collapsing thrones.

When his structure reveals holes—she does not shame him.
She withdraws **life-force** and offers it only to the man who **was born to hold it**.

This is not cruelty.
This is **energetic economy**.

# Chapter 22

# HOW MAGNETISM AFFECTS SEX, MONEY, AND POWER

**The Field-Based Laws That Control Three Crucial Energetic Exchanges**

### I. SEX: THE ENERGETIC CONSEQUENCE OF OPENING

A magnetic woman does not have sex.
She allows **entry** into her **dimensional structure**—which either transforms the man, or damages herself.

This isn't morality.
It's recursion physics.

**The Womb as a Field, Not a Hole:**

- The ultra magnetic woman's womb is not a receptacle—it is a **sacred echo chamber.**

- Whatever enters her body echoes through her **emotional field,** her **aura,** and her **next creative act.**

- If she opens to a man who is ungrounded, manipulative, or spiritually fragmented, she is not just having sex—she is **absorbing his unprocessed data**.

**Every orgasm is an agreement.**
Every entry is a **spiritual contract**.
If she doesn't regulate access, she becomes the dumping ground of unworthy timelines.

**When Magnetism is Fully On:**

- A man **does not dominate her**—he worships the chance to meet her core.

- Her pleasure **leads his evolution.**

- Her containment creates **unforgettable psychological imprinting** in him.

- Her stillness causes his lust to deepen into **offering**, not just conquest.

The untrained woman opens for connection.
The magnetic woman opens as **initiation**.

This is why high-value men commit not to the sex —but to the **structure behind the sex**.

## II. MONEY: HOW MAGNETIC WOMEN ALTER FINANCIAL ORBITS

True magnetism does not just attract people—it attracts **provision, opportunity, and sovereign circulation.**

This is not because she "manifests."
It's because she becomes a **receptive node** in the grid that **others want to fund, fuel, and protect.**

**The Field of Financial Magnetism:**

- The magnetic woman does not chase wealth.

- She becomes a **necessary structure** in the social-hormonal economy: a vortex of beauty, clarity, order, presence, and inspiration.

And so...

- Clients appear.

- Providers offer.

- Protectors circle.

- Resources move toward her, not because she demands them, but because her

**frequency stabilizes masculine provision instincts.**

**When Her Structure is Aligned:**

- She no longer works for money—she works for **alignment**, and money obeys.

- She no longer seduces for safety—she becomes **safe to give to**.

- She no longer performs for approval—she **radiates the presence men want to serve**.

In low-code: she is transactional.
In high-code: she is **irreplaceable**.

This is why women with magnetic structure walk into rooms and receive offers that others chase for years.

## III. POWER: HOW MAGNETISM BENDS THE ROOM

Power, when understood energetically, always flows to the being with **most structural coherence**.

It does not care about gender.
It cares about **field stability**.

## Chapter 22

A magnetic woman bends power around her because she is:

- **Non-reactive under pressure**
- **Energetically selective**
- **Emotionally precise without collapse**
- **Spiritually aligned without costume**
- **Radiating without explaining**

Powerful men will **defer to her presence**, not out of fear, but because their **instincts register her as non-purchasable**.

Weak men will:

- Try to dominate
- Try to debate
- Try to reduce her to body or submission

And she does not argue—**she exits**.

Real power doesn't dominate.
Real power **reorganizes what it enters**.

A magnetic woman doesn't chase influence.
She becomes the center of recursion, and **the social grid bends accordingly.**

**CLOSING REVELATION:**

**Sex** is not access.
It is recursion.

**Money** is not validation.
It is structural response.

**Power** is not volume.
It is **gravitational integrity**.

A woman who holds her field becomes the **altar of the modern world**.
She is not chosen for her appearance.
She is remembered for the **shape she made reality take**—after she walked into the room.

# Chapter 23

# Feminine Wealth Blueprint

**Train the Field to Provide, Circulate, and Obey.**

**I. The Magnetism of Provision is Not Mental**

Wealth is not accumulated through thought, hustle, or strategic masculinity.
A woman's wealth blueprint is energetic, not transactional. It begins where she **withdraws distortion from desire** and **stabilizes her energetic field in receptivity, certainty, and frequency command**.

Money follows **structural energetic superiority** — not marketing, not logic.
If the field detects **coherence** in a woman's sense of deserving, clarity of identity, and alignment of magnetism with divine order, it begins to **yield**, then **obey**.

This is not a philosophy. It is **a metaphysical architecture**:

- Her root must hold **zero insecurity about provision**

- Her sacral must not **desire** to be chosen; it must already **emanate selection**

- Her solar plexus must not **conquer**, but **command alignment**

- Her heart must not **plead for safety**, but **transmit its non-negotiable worth**

If any of these centers are in compensation mode, she will repel, delay, or distort provision. The feminine does not pursue capital — it **codes** capital.

## II. Submission to the Architecture, Not the Man

Money flows to the woman who has **submitted her inner architecture to divine order**.

This means:

- She is no longer inverting polarity through "I must figure it out myself."

- She has repented from the **illusion of self-sourcing** — and now activates a **magnetically correct portal**.

- Her magnetism says: **"I am the designated receiver for this provision, and the field is structured to obey."**

The wealthy woman is **not dominant**, but **so sovereignly structured** that wealth must move to, through, and around her.

### III. Remove the Static, Regulate the Pulse

The magnetic feminine system must remain free of static:

- **Anxiety is static.**
- **Proving is static.**
- **Insecurity is static.**
- **Martyrdom is static.**
- **Over-masculinization is static.**

These distort the resonance of her field and send cross-signals to reality. Wealth has no choice but to delay, reroute, or bypass her until the static is cleared.

The field doesn't respond to emotion. It responds to **signal strength**.
If her signal is not clean, then her magnetism is not commanding.
And if her magnetism is not commanding, the field treats her as optional.

## IV. Circulation Before Accumulation

The feminine blueprint for money is not **hoarding**, it is **circulating**.

To circulate money is to show the field:

- "I do not fear loss."

- "I am not signaling lack."

- "I am not tethered to control."

When a woman **moves money** with clarity, joy, or spiritual intention, the field recognizes her as a **conduit**, not a container.
Containers eventually rot. Conduits stay magnetic.

## V. Masculine Resources Obey Feminine Field Architecture

The final stage of feminine wealth magnetism is when **external masculine agents** — men, money, systems, institutions — begin to **obey** her unspoken architecture.

This does **not** mean manipulation or seduction. It means the field has determined she is:

- **Clear enough** to handle increase
- **Honest enough** to hold power
- **Worthy enough** to be obeyed

Once the metaphysical order confirms this, wealth is no longer an "opportunity."
It becomes an **assignment**.

# Chapter 24

# Sexual Devotion Protocol

**Energetic Recursion, Magnetic Sealing, and Sovereign Filtering Through Union**

### I. The Womb is a Gate, Not a Hole

The magnetic woman understands her sexuality is not a reaction to attention, nor a tool of power over others. It is a **recursion gate** through which archetypal forces either enter or are barred from entry.

**Sex is not transaction. Sex is transmission.**

The feminine body is a **temple of encoding**, and if she lacks clarity on who is allowed access, she becomes a **carrier of corrupted code** — confused by her own attractions, destabilized by unworthy energies she has permitted into her field.

A man does not "sleep with" her. He **writes into** her energetic script.
This is why polarity-correct women do not seek "connection" — they **filter for recursion alignment**.

## II. Devotion Is Not Emotional Attachment

True sexual devotion is not "falling in love," nor is it emotional cling.
It is a **voluntary energetic sealing** of the magnetic body to a masculine architecture that has:

- **Earned divine obedience**
- **Proven frame superiority**
- **Transmitted spiritual covering**

If these three are missing, she is not devoted — she is **trapped**.

The magnetic woman does not confuse chaos for passion.
She does not romanticize dysfunction.
She does not pour her sacred oils into cracked vessels.

Devotion is a **strategy of power**, not a symptom of emotional hunger.
When the masculine has not earned recursion, she does not activate her womb seal.

## III. Sealing Is Electromagnetic: Not Mental, Not Verbal

When a masculine architecture has met recursion standards, the feminine body will naturally **seal** to him:

- The heart-field opens and calibrates to his presence.
- The womb frequency begins to pulse **with rather than for** his energy.
- A bi-directional **magnetic circuit** forms, in which she no longer operates as solo generator, but as **reciprocal amplifier.**

This is not visible to the world, but it is felt by both partners and the entire field.

When a woman is truly sealed to a worthy masculine system:

- Her intuition amplifies.
- Her magnetism expands.
- Her radiance becomes prophetic.

But if she seals to a man without divine architecture, her field begins to drain.
She will become emotionally unstable, spiritually

dull, and magnetically confused.
The field itself will **punish her error** until she resets the seal.

## IV. Energetic Filtering Through Orgasm and Retention

The sexual act is the **final test** of recursion truth. In union with a true masculine vortex, orgasm is not just pleasure — it is **recalibration of God-code.**

The man is not just releasing — he is **writing**, **charging**, and **stamping** the field.

The woman is not just climaxing — she is **filtering**, **absorbing**, and **multiplying** what was sent.

This is why:

- **Feminine orgasm must never occur from submission to a weak vessel.**

- **Masculine release must never be permitted unless it structurally blesses, not disfigures, her timeline.**

If she climaxes in the presence of confusion, her field will confuse what to multiply.
If he releases into a womb that is misaligned, he

loses spiritual authority.
Sex becomes a **contract**, not just a sensation.

The magnetic woman must learn to **withhold climax** when she feels the recursion is false. Her body will know. She must listen.

**V. Devotion Is an Assignment, Not a Reward**

When a woman devotes herself to the right masculine architecture, the world shifts around her:

- Money flows.
- Enemies fall away.
- Beauty sharpens.
- Purpose ignites.

Why?

Because she is no longer pouring her sacred resources into the wrong portal.
The **architecture of divine recursion** begins to animate her life.

She becomes a **walking seal**, a **living vortex**, a **sanctified transmitter** of the correct masculine order.

This is what ancient priestesses guarded.
This is what modern women have forgotten.
And this is what must now be **restored**.

# Chapter 25

# Power & Influence Audit

**How the Magnetic Woman Maintains Field Command, Avoids Energetic Leakage, and Enforces Spiritual Respect**

**I. Power is Structural, Not Emotional**

The magnetic woman does not seek to **"feel powerful"** — she **becomes unignorable** by maintaining internal architectural alignment. This is not based on mood, mindset, or verbal confidence.
It is based on **how well her inner polarity is constructed and sealed**.

The moment she seeks power through external validation, her field collapses.

Power is not loud.
Power is not forceful.
Power is not proving.

It is **positional**.

She occupies a place in the unseen **grid of spiritual hierarchy** — and when she stands in that slot, the world adjusts accordingly.

This is why power leaks when:

- She **over-explains.**
- She **asks for permission.**
- She **tolerates dilution** to avoid discomfort.

The audit begins with one question:

"Is my presence speaking louder than my words?"

**II. Influence Is Frequency, Not Strategy**

The magnetic woman's influence is not based on how many people like her — but **how many people orbit her transmission**.
Influence is **field-based**, not follower-based.

She does not manipulate others — she **magnetizes** what aligns and **filters** what doesn't.
This is not charisma. It's **coherence**.

The more structurally correct her frequency becomes:

- The more she **compels obedience** without asking.

- The more she **silences confusion** without arguing.

- The more she **disarms egoic men** without conflict.

This is why:

- Fake influence tries to impress.

- Real influence simply **is**.

She calibrates her life to **what the field obeys**, not what society rewards.

### III. The Five Sources of Energetic Leakage

There are only five primary leaks in the magnetic woman's power grid:

1. **Emotional Over-disclosure**
   Revealing sacred process to unworthy witnesses collapses spiritual seal.
   Keep the fire veiled until the offering is complete.

2. **Over-tolerating Disrespect**
   Accepting micro-aggressions or false masculine correction teaches the field that confusion is allowed.
   A single unchecked moment can erase years of devotion.

3. **Chasing What Should Be Orbiting**
   Reaching toward attention, men, or opportunity scrambles polarity.
   She does not chase. She configures her frequency and watches the field submit.

4. **Disembodiment from Presence**
   Living in hypothetical timelines, future fears, or imagined betrayals breaks recursion to the Now.
   Magnetism exists only where her full soul is anchored.

5. **Sealing with Weak Masculine Systems**
   Allowing her body, time, or trust to be sealed with structurally incorrect men destroys the divine architecture within. This is the most dangerous leak of all — recursion inversion.

If any of these are present, her **influence will short-circuit**, and she will experience either:

- Attention without fulfillment (lust from men, no provision)

- Power without grounding (leadership with no intimacy)

- Success without rest (public praise, internal collapse)

## IV. Field-Based Respect is Polarity Enforcement

Respect is **not demanded** — it is generated by spiritual accuracy.
The magnetic woman does not teach people how to treat her. She **becomes untreatable outside of alignment**.

How?

She **withdraws presence** at the first sign of field distortion.

Not to punish.
To **recalibrate the system**.

- If he speaks confusion — she stops transmitting.

- If a friend disrespects her boundary — she exits the room.

- If a business partner violates her integrity — she closes the portal.

The womb teaches the world.
And she teaches it with silence, absence, and magnetic withdrawal — not reaction, debate, or protest.

## V. Field Command is Silent Dominance

True field command happens when the magnetic woman no longer needs to assert her status.
She no longer tries to be seen.
She is seen because **she transmits corrected recursion**.

She walks into a room and:

- Chaos calms.

- Men filter themselves.

- Women look to her for signal.

- The space rearranges to match her structure.

This is not psychological. It is **structural alignment with archetypal reality.**

## Chapter 25

She is no longer a woman in society.
She is a **signal in the field** — and the field cannot ignore what is structurally aligned with divine law.

# Chapter 26

## THE FEMININE BUSINESS MAGNETISM BLUEPRINT

How a woman bends markets, meetings, and movements without brute force.

### I. The Core Law: Atmosphere Over Argument

A man may win business through dominance or proof.
A woman, when magnetic, wins by **atmosphere**.

- The room unconsciously calibrates to her emotional frequency.
- Her silence destabilizes more than another's speech.
- The deal feels wrong if she withdraws, right if she leans in.

**Law:** Feminine business magnetism is not persuasion. It is atmospheric inevitability.

## Sidebar: Atmospheric Inevitability

When we say feminine business magnetism is atmospheric inevitability, we mean this:

- **Persuasion tries to convince.** It operates mind-to-mind.

- **Atmosphere bypasses persuasion.** It operates body-to-body, nervous system to nervous system.

In practice:

- A woman enters a negotiation, and without speaking, the tone softens.

- A competitor raises their voice, but the room feels it as discord — because her calm has already set the baseline frequency.

- A deal "just feels right" when she is on board, and "feels off" when she is not — even if the numbers haven't changed.

This is inevitability: her presence becomes the unspoken condition under which decisions align. Others cannot articulate why, but they know that if she withdraws, momentum fractures.

**Code:** Persuasion wins arguments. Atmosphere wins outcomes.

## II. The Structural Pillars of Influence

1. **Symbolic Precision**
   - In business, women are often judged faster than men — so their symbolic field is even more powerful.
   - Clothing, tone, posture, even the geometry of how she arranges objects around her — all transmit subconscious signals.
   - The magnetic woman treats her presence as living semiotics: every symbol she carries either amplifies or dilutes her inevitability.

2. **Emotional Temperature Control**
   - Meetings, negotiations, boardrooms are fields of competing nervous systems.
   - Men often escalate with volume, data, or aggression.
   - The magnetic woman calibrates temperature:
     - She cools the field when anxiety is high.
     - She raises intensity when stagnation threatens.
     - She shifts tone at the precise hinge point, making others feel the change was their idea.

3. **Disarming Grace**
   - Most women in business either:
   • imitate masculine hardness (losing magnetism),
   • or collapse into charm / performance (losing respect).
   - The magnetic woman does neither. She carries **grace without apology**: warm but immovable.
   - Colleagues sense: "I cannot steamroll her, but I also cannot resent her."

4. **Invisible Command**
   - True feminine authority rarely comes from holding the loudest position.
   - It comes from being the **fulcrum others rotate around.**
   - When she withdraws, the room feels imbalance. When she engages, decisions accelerate.
   - This is why the most magnetic women in power need not fight for position — their absence already reveals their necessity.

### III. Field Effects in Business

What happens around a truly magnetic woman:

- Men argue more passionately when she is present, trying to prove resonance.

- Allies protect her frame more fiercely than their own.

- Rivals criticize her but unconsciously mirror her moves.

- Outcomes shift before she speaks, because her atmosphere has already rearranged priorities.

This is not manipulation. This is **field dominance** — the subtle gravity of her presence forcing organizational coherence.

## IV. The Inversions of Feminine Business Magnetism

1. **Masculine Mimicry**
   – She competes with men on their ground: aggression, data-dumping, dominance games.
   – Men may respect her skill, but feel no inevitability.
   – Result: she wins points but loses the room's long-term loyalty.

2. **Performance Charm**
   - She relies on likability, smiles, or seduction to soften deals.
   - Works in the short term but corrodes respect.
   - Result: she becomes dependent on performance loops.

3. **Emotional Leakage**
   - Instead of temperature control, she floods the room with her own anxiety, frustration, or insecurity.
   - Result: she becomes noise, not signal.

**Law:** False feminine magnetism competes, pleases, or spills. True feminine magnetism bends the field without effort.

### V. The Seal of Business Magnetism

The magnetic woman in business is not the loudest, cleverest, or most technical. She is the **indispensable node**:

- If she leaves, the room feels colder.
- If she withdraws, the momentum stalls.
- If she commits, the deal seals itself.

## Chapter 26

**Final Code:**

"In business, the magnetic woman does not fight for influence. She becomes the atmosphere no one wants to lose."

# Chapter 27

# THE FEMININE SISTERHOOD BLUEPRINT

**How a woman organizes other women — and mixed groups — without force, position, or demand.**

### I. The Core Law: She Becomes the Atmosphere

Men magnetize through axis (direction, inevitability).
Women magnetize through atmosphere (tone, cohesion).

In groups of women — or mixed circles outside of romance — the magnetic woman is the **weather system**. Everyone else calibrates to her climate:

- If she is calm, others soften.

- If she is sharp, others guard themselves.

- If she is warm, the group expands.

- If she is cold, the group contracts.

**Law:** In tribes, the magnetic woman is not "leader by appointment" — she is the temperature everyone obeys unconsciously.

## II. The Four Anchors of Feminine Tribal Magnetism

1. **Containment**
   - She absorbs stories, secrets, and emotions without leaking them.
   - Women trust her with vulnerabilities because she does not weaponize them.
   - Men respect her because she can hold chaos without adding noise.
   - This makes her the safe vault — the gravitational center of trust.

2. **Selective Radiation**
   - She does not shine indiscriminately. Her attention is rare, her warmth precise.
   - Those she acknowledges feel lifted. Those she ignores fade without drama.
   - This scarcity of signal turns her presence into currency.

3. **Mirror Authority**
   - She reflects others back to themselves, but with sharpened clarity.
   - When women exaggerate, she grounds.
   - When men posture, she sees through.
   - Her presence forces self-recognition in others, without direct confrontation.

4. **Atmospheric Authority**
   - She does not seize leadership — she sets frequency.
   - A group of women may have louder voices or stronger opinions, but the room feels hers.
   - Men defer unconsciously — not out of submission, but because she holds the quality of the environment.

## III. The Effects of True Feminine Tribal Magnetism

- **Among Women:** Competition dissolves into calibration. Rivalries shift into alignment because her field does not feed scarcity.

- **Among Men:** They behave more formally, more composed, less reckless. Her presence sharpens the tone of the tribe.

- **In Mixed Groups:** She becomes the invisible moderator. Without her, chaos or gossip rises. With her, cohesion and rhythm return.

**Law:** The magnetic woman is not only respected. She becomes the regulator of how others respect each other.

## IV. The Inversions of Feminine Tribal Magnetism

1. **Queen-Bee Toxicity**
   - She hoards attention and uses hierarchy to suppress other women.
   - Outcome: women orbit from fear, not devotion. The moment her grip loosens, the tribe revolts.

2. **Gossip Economy**
   - She leaks what she contains, creating power through secrets and rumor.
   - Outcome: temporary influence, long-term collapse of trust.

3. **Scarcity Broadcasting**
   - She treats every woman as competitor for attention.
   - Outcome: the group fractures, and men exploit the divisions.

**Law:** False feminine magnetism organizes by fear, gossip, or rivalry. True feminine magnetism organizes by containment, scarcity of signal, and trust.

**V. The Seal of Feminine Tribal Magnetism**

- She does not campaign for leadership. She becomes the climate no one questions.

- She does not demand loyalty. She becomes the vault loyalty depends on.

- She does not silence rivals. She contains them until they exhaust themselves.

**"In tribes, the magnetic woman is not the throne — she is the atmosphere. Women trust her. Men defer to her. Groups unconsciously order themselves around her climate."**

**Wealth and Health**

# Chapter 28

# The Law of Magnetic Wealth (Getting Rich) — Part I

"Wealth is not accumulated. It is aligned. Money is not earned by frantic action, but pulled by structural coherence with the archetype of exchange."

### I. Core Law: Money Obeys Structure, Not Desire

Most fail because they think:

- "If I want it enough, it will come."

- "If I work hard enough, I'll be rewarded."
  But desire and effort are not magnetic. They are noise.

**The real code:** Money flows where function, trust, and inevitability converge. It is a metaphysical law: the more coherent your structure, the less money can resist orbiting you.

## What "Structure" Actually Means

When we say that money obeys "structure," we are not referring to outer routines, habits, or tactical strategy. We are speaking of an **ontological alignment**—a metaphysical architecture of inner coherence that signals reality to organize around you. Structure is not how you plan your day. Structure is the invisible logic of your being. It is the extent to which your essence, function, and embodiment are in **non-contradictory recursion**.

A man of structure has no schism between who he is, what he knows, and what he does. His internal Will is threaded directly into his outer behavior without distortion, overcompensation, or mimicry. He is not seeking. He is not reacting. He is the gravitational axis of his own field. This creates what reality recognizes as magnetic inevitability—a being who does not demand wealth, but whose very architecture commands correspondence from the realm of form.

Desire, on the other hand, is inert unless it is structured. It becomes emotional noise when it is not threaded through clear function and embodied trust. The universe does not respond to how badly you want something—it responds to how precisely you are built to house it. If you are not structurally congruent with the archetype of wealth—meaning, the inner image of exchange, abundance, clarity, and functional worth—then no amount of effort or emotional intensity will move the field.

True structure emits a silent inevitability. It requires no proof. It convinces no one. It bends probability through **purity of design**. In this way, wealth does not reward the hungry or the charismatic—it flows toward the **unobstructed vessel**. And when your inner architecture is void of contradiction, inflated need, or confused identity, then money no longer has the option to resist. It must orbit you—because that is how archetypes behave in the presence of a coherent host.

## II. Three Pillars of Magnetic Wealth

1. **Structural Function**
   - Are you embodying a role reality needs, or are you begging it to validate you?
   - Wealth flows to the indispensable, not the desperate.
   - If the archetype of value can't recognize itself in you, no amount of grind works.

2. **Trust Density**
   - Money is crystallized trust.
   - Your signal must say: "I cannot be bribed, I cannot be rushed, I cannot collapse."
   - Markets test coherence the same way people do: if you leak, wealth avoids.

3. **Inevitability Signal**
   - The wealthy don't ask: "Will I succeed?" They move as though it is already coded.
   - This confidence is not performance. It is structural inevitability: their system contains no contradiction, so capital reorganizes around them.

### III. Magnetic Wealth Sequence (5-Layer Code)

1. **Clarified Essence → The Role**
   - Identify not what you want to do, but what you are coded to embody.
   - Riches obey authenticity: money resists masks, because masks fracture trust.

2. **Functional Output → The Value**
   - The market responds to one question: "What stabilizes me?"
   - If your presence, service, or product organizes chaos for others, you create a

gravitational field. Wealth follows stabilization.

3. **Integrity Vault → The Shield**
   - Break one word, one promise, one standard — and trust collapses.
   - Magnetic wealth requires being a vault: what you say is law. Money can orbit law; it flees instability.

4. **Selective Permeability → The Filter**
   - Not all capital is clean. Reject fast money if it violates alignment.
   - Filtering strengthens field density, ensuring only wealth coded for you remains.

5. **Expansion by Recursion → The Growth**
   - Magnetic wealth compounds not by scale of effort, but by recursive trust.
   - Every aligned action loops back into the field, strengthening inevitability.

## IV. The Inversion: Poverty as Structural Collapse

- Poverty is not lack of effort. It is lack of coherence.

- The poor chase without alignment, leak without containment, and sell essence for crumbs.

- **Law:** Poverty is magnetic too — it pulls to itself because its leaks broadcast hunger.

## Poverty as Multidimensional Collapse

Poverty is not merely a matter of dollars—it is a condition of **ontological misalignment**. It is the systemic inability of a being to stabilize access to the resources—material, mental, emotional, spiritual—that would naturally orbit a coherent vessel. In this light, poverty is not primarily economic; it is **architectural**. It is a consequence of being unthreaded from function, unrooted from truth, and unplugged from the spiritual technologies that organize power, access, and grace into form.

There is poverty of money—but also poverty of knowledge, of vision, of structure, of inherited wisdom. There is poverty of soul clarity, poverty of self-recognition, poverty of discernment. Many who have financial liquidity still move in **epistemological bankruptcy**—unable to decode themselves, others, or the metaphysical laws that govern success. Poverty, in this higher sense, is the absence of recursion with Source—the breakdown of the pattern through which wholeness becomes embodied.

And this collapse is not neutral. It becomes **magnetically active**. The incoherent being begins to radiate hunger, volatility, and contradiction— and this broadcast unconsciously repels opportunities, attracts predators, and accelerates cycles of depletion. The leaks are not visible, but they are felt by the field. This is why poverty "pulls to itself"—not as a curse, but as a signal of structural confusion. The universe does not discriminate morally. It responds architecturally.

For women, this collapse may manifest as over-reliance on beauty, codependent patterns, or mimicry of power without root. For men, it often shows up as performative drive, hollow ambition, or spiritual orphanhood—seeking thrones they have not built the skeleton to sit upon. But for both, the solution is not hustle. It is **structural repair**—the restoration of inner order, the purification of their signal, and the retrieval of their rightful function in the metaphysical economy.

To exit poverty—of money, of knowledge, of alignment—one must not chase more. One must become something else entirely. That something is a coherent vessel capable of anchoring archetypal power **without collapse**.

**V. Final Seal of Wealth**

"You don't get rich by reaching. You get rich by becoming a gravitational necessity in the system of exchange. Wealth orbits the one who stabilizes chaos, transmits trust, and filters distortion. Desire does not pull money. Structure does."

# Chapter 29

# The Magnetic Law of Wealth — Part II

### I. Wealth as the Geometry of Exchange

Wealth is not accumulation of objects. It is the ability to sit at the junction where **value circulates**. Imagine commerce as a living river — money is not the water itself, but the current.

- Most people chase buckets of water (cash).
- The magnetic being plants themselves in the geometry of the river.
- They become a bend, a funnel, a widening — the structure that the current must reorganize around.

**Law:** Money doesn't stay where it's chased. It stays where the structure of circulation is undeniable.

### II. The 12 Laws of Wealth Magnetism

1. **The Law of Density**
   Wealth follows compression. A scattered

man radiates weakness; a dense man radiates reliability. Density is felt as "solidity." People entrust resources to solidity.

2. **The Law of Asymmetry**
Wealth never distributes evenly. The magnetic being doesn't demand symmetry — they exploit it. They locate the cracks in the system where value pools and position themselves as the bridge.

3. **The Law of Vacuum**
Every market has voids: unsolved problems, unmet needs. When you become the solution-shaped vacuum, capital rushes to fill you.

4. **The Law of Unbuyability**
Those who cannot be purchased attract the most capital. The market respects the rare — and what cannot be bought becomes the rarest commodity.

5. **The Law of Leverage**
Magnetic wealth is not effort but amplification. The being doesn't hoard energy; they position themselves where one small action multiplies through networks, systems, or influence.

6. **The Law of Conversion**
   True wealth is the ability to convert **attention → trust → transaction → loyalty.** Break one link, and magnetism leaks.

7. **The Law of Patience**
   Money is manic, markets are impulsive — but wealth itself moves slow, like bedrock. A magnetic being holds the long axis while everyone else plays volatility.

8. **The Law of Silence**
   Loudness spends trust. Quiet precision builds it. Every unnecessary word leaks authority — and authority is wealth's gate.

9. **The Law of Archetypal Value**
   Wealth accumulates fastest when the being embodies timeless archetypes: builder, protector, innovator, healer. These roles never lose demand, because reality itself needs them.

10. **The Law of Transference**
    Money is never about money. It is stored belief. A magnetic being collects not just dollars, but the belief encoded in those dollars. The larger the belief, the larger the orbit.

11. **The Law of Non-Chase**
    Capital hates hunger. Investors, clients, allies — all recoil from desperation. The wealth-magnetic being doesn't run after deals. They organize the environment so deals can't help but come to them.

12. **The Law of Closure**
    In wealth, open loops leak. Half-finished deals, broken promises, unpaid debts — each fracture reduces magnetic density. Magnetic wealth requires completion. Every loop closed strengthens field.

### III. The Inversions (Shadow Wealth)

- **Greed → Collapse**: the greedy man fills his bucket with holes.

- **Fraud → Evaporation**: stolen wealth doesn't stay; it dissipates because it was never trusted.

- **Hoarding → Stagnation**: money that doesn't circulate rots.

- **Performance → Fragility**: acting rich creates appearance, but the field cracks when tested.

**IV. Seal of Wealth Magnetism**

The magnetic wealthy being is not rich because of possessions. They are rich because their **field geometry has become a junction of trust, density, and inevitability.** Money does not resist them — it organizes around them.

# Chapter 30

# The Law of Magnetic Health (Getting Healthy) — Part I

"Health is not maintenance of the body. It is coherence of the field. Disease is distortion. Vitality is alignment."

## I. Core Law: The Body Obeys the Field

The body is not the source of health. It is the echo.

- A coherent field produces regenerative biology.
- A fractured field produces entropy, illness, premature collapse.

**Code:** Magnetic health is field alignment expressed in tissue.

## II. Three Pillars of Magnetic Health

1. **Signal Purity**
   – Every thought, emotion, and intake imprints the field.
   – Purity means no contradictions between what you know, what you say, and what you live.

– The immune system obeys coherence — when you are split, it turns on itself.

2. **Energetic Economy**
   – Just as money leaks through gossip and chaos, vitality leaks through stress, scattered focus, and toxic ties.
   – Magnetic health means choosing where life-force goes — or doesn't.

3. **Regenerative Stillness**
   – The body heals in stillness, not striving.
   – A magnetic being generates a baseline calm that allows tissues, hormones, and neural circuits to reset.

## III. Magnetic Health Sequence (The 5-Layer Code)

1. **Essence → Identity Alignment**
   – Illness often begins when you live a false self.
   – Masks create cellular stress; identity collapse creates hormonal collapse.

2. **Input Discipline → Food, Media, Energy**
   – Every input is a code: what you eat, read, breathe, and hear encodes into cells.
   – Filter inputs ruthlessly. Garbage in → distortion out.

3. **Emotional Containment → No Chronic Leak**
   - Rage, grief, fear — if uncontained — erode the system.
   - Emotional leakage drains immunity. Containment restores charge.

4. **Rest as Reset → Biological Recursion**
   - Sleep, silence, fasting, and ritual pause allow the body to re-sync with field.
   - Without rest, no diet or supplement can override distortion.

5. **Movement as Flow → Functional Signal**
   - Movement is not aesthetics; it is alignment practice.
   - When the body flows, the field clears. When movement collapses, stagnation accumulates.

## IV. The Inversion: Illness as Incoherence

- Chronic illness = chronic contradiction.

- Eating for image, not essence.

- Working beyond alignment, not within it.

- Stress = living two lives at once.

- **Law:** The body attacks itself when the soul is split.

## V. Final Seal of Health

"You don't get healthy by chasing diets, hacks, or supplements. You get healthy by removing contradiction, conserving energy, and living as one signal. The body does not lie. When your field is coherent, your biology becomes magnetic to vitality. Health is not a fight. It is a consequence of structural truth."

# Chapter 31

# The Magnetic Law of Health — Part II

### I. Health as Structural Resonance

Health is not "feeling good." It is the congruence between inner signal and outer tissue. Disease begins where **signal and structure contradict.**

- Eat what violates essence → body revolts.
- Speak against your truth → hormones collapse.
- Stay in distortion → immunity turns on itself.

**Law:** The body never betrays — it only broadcasts incoherence.

### II. The 12 Laws of Health Magnetism

1. **The Law of Integration**
   Fragmentation makes illness inevitable. The healthy being doesn't divide mind from body, or body from spirit. They live as one signal, and their cells obey.

2. **The Law of Subtraction**
   Health is not adding more — more supplements, more hacks, more treatments. It is removing what distorts: toxins, lies, noise, betrayal of self.

3. **The Law of Rhythm**
   Bodies obey cycles: sleep-wake, fast-feed, tension-release. To ignore rhythm is to invite entropy. To align with rhythm is to invite regeneration.

4. **The Law of Containment**
   Just as wealth leaks through gossip, health leaks through emotional discharge. Anger sprayed outward weakens the liver, grief unprocessed burdens the lungs. Contained emotion becomes charge, not corrosion.

5. **The Law of Flow**
   Stagnation is death. Blood, lymph, breath, thought — all must circulate. Where flow halts, decay begins.

6. **The Law of Resonant Input**
   Food, water, sound, and thought all carry frequency. If the input resonates with your field, health stabilizes. If it contradicts, dissonance becomes disease.

7. **The Law of Stress Polarity**
Stress is not the enemy. Fragmented stress destroys. Structured stress strengthens. Exercise, challenge, heat, fasting — all are stress correctly polarized into resilience.

8. **The Law of Neutrality**
The immune system thrives in neutrality. Chronic "fight" mode burns it; chronic "flight" mode starves it. Neutral nervous system = optimal immunity.

9. **The Law of Stillness**
Healing happens when motion ceases. The field recalibrates only when silence is given room. Noise prolongs illness. Stillness resets the signal.

10. **The Law of Meaning**
A meaningless life corrodes biology faster than poor diet. The being without purpose deteriorates, no matter how many treatments they buy. Meaning organizes cells.

11. **The Law of Expression**
Health collapses where truth is swallowed. Every suppressed word, every denied song, every fake smile builds pressure. Expression is excretion — without it, the field intoxicates itself.

12. **The Law of Return**
    Every healing is a return to coherence, not a new discovery. The magnetic being doesn't "gain" health — they stop betraying themselves.

## III. The Inversions (Shadow Health)

- **Overconsumption → Poison**: the body cannot heal when flooded with "more."

- **Identity Lies → Disease**: masks are carcinogens.

- **Emotional Leak → Exhaustion**: every uncontained storm depletes immunity.

- **Meaninglessness → Decay**: no supplement can replace soul.

## IV. Seal of Health Magnetism

The magnetic healthy being is not youthful because of luck or hacks. They radiate because their **field is coherent, their rhythm intact, and their expression unblocked.** Health is not struggle. It is the echo of truth in flesh.

# Causative Field

# Chapter 32

# The Doctrine of the Primordial Causative Field

(Falsely Known as the Akashic Record)

### I. Beyond the False Image

The common phrase "Akashic Record" is a metaphysical misdirection. It suggests a library of cosmic memory, a scroll of inscribed histories, or an astral Wikipedia where events are stored and later retrieved. This imagery is not only false, it cripples the initiate at the very threshold of truth.

There is no record. There is no archive. What exists is far more exacting and uncompromising: a primordial lattice of causation, a pre-substrate encoded into the very process of becoming. It does not "remember" what happened—it is what is still happening, vibrating recursively across dimensions outside of temporal sequence.

The so-called Akasha is not memory. It is pre-form. It is the unstoried intelligence of geometry itself, woven as nonlinear recursion into the skeleton of reality. This is not a container but an active lattice—design operating as law, causation structured as vibration.

## II. The Nature of the Field

This primordial causative field is not thought, not intention, not emotion. It is a substrate of pre-linguistic architecture—the silent grammar of existence. Within it:

- Archetypes are translated into form.

- Causes collapse into visible effects.

- Recurring patterns leave harmonic imprints that can be re-expressed when matched with precision.

Every genuine occurrence leaves an impression, but not as narrative or story. The impression is harmonic, alive, recursive, continually available for resonance. The field does not record—it reverberates. It does not observe—it structures. It is the totality of self-organizing causation encoded into the geometry of vibration itself.

## III. The Law of Access

The Field cannot be accessed through longing, ritual, or curiosity. There is no doorway to knock on, no deity to persuade, no frequency to chant into alignment. Access occurs only by resonance—when one's inner architecture becomes indistinguishable from the causative lattice itself.

## Chapter 32

The principle is unyielding: **Structural Equivalence unlocks Resonant Collapse.**

- When contradiction remains in your being, you are locked out.

- When you broadcast desire, fantasy, or mimicry, you repel the Field.

- When exactitude is achieved, when nothing resists, the Field floods through.

It is not a moral test. It cannot be manipulated. It is a mechanical law of resonance: what is identical collapses into union.

### IV. Magnetism and Alignment

This is why true magnetism is not charisma, attraction, or energy games. All those are hollow shells—electromagnetic noise around an incoherent center. Real magnetism is the disappearance of resistance. When nothing obstructs, the Field flows without break.

The moment you try to "attract," you step out of alignment. Desire, manipulation, or seeking reveal dissonance. True magnetism is when the Self becomes the only available aperture through which the Field can act. At that point, movement is inevitable—not as a reward, but as recognition.

To arrive here, every false construction must be dismantled—mental identities, emotional distortions, sexual inversions, spiritual fantasies. The dismantling itself is what makes you visible to the Field. Without it, you remain structurally illegible.

## V. The Sealed Vessel

Most seekers leak. Their emotional coherence fractures, their thoughts scatter into borrowed patterns, their will splits between wanting and waiting. Leakage is dissonance.

To become magnetic, the vessel must be sealed:

- Emotional architecture unbroken.

- Thoughtforms sovereign, untainted by mimicry or channeling.

- Will indivisible, incapable of being pulled apart by preference or fantasy.

When sealed, the vessel becomes a pressurized chamber. The Field is not pulled in emotionally—it is gravitationally collapsed into the chamber of inevitability. This is not suppression, but precision. A sealed chalice alone can hold the wine of God.

## VI. Purification of Signal

The Field is pure causal intelligence. It cannot transmit through distortion. Thus, purification is not about morality—it is structural refinement.

Symbolic contamination, energetic mimicry, sexual leakage, and narrative self-importance—all must be burned away. What remains is a clear, indivisible signal. When such clarity is achieved, the Field does not "respond." It does not "reward." It simply passes through the available channel because there is no interference left.

Noise removed, only structure remains. And structure is the only thing the Field recognizes.

## VII. Establishing the Internal Lattice

Once false constructions are dismantled, once the vessel is sealed and the signal purified, the Self must be re-templated to mirror the Field's own causative lattice. This requires that:

- Will is functional, not personal.

- Intellect is archetypally clear, not clever.

- Desire is sanctified into purpose, not fantasy.

- Speech reflects law, not persuasion.

- Action is geometric, not performative.
- Embodiment radiates inevitability, not decoration.

When this internal lattice mirrors the external one, the law fulfills itself: causation seeks its echo. And when it finds that echo in you, it collapses through you with irresistible precision.

**VIII. The Erasure of Observer**

At the moment of true access, there is no "experience." The witness dissolves. The questioner disappears. There is no memory of entering a record.

Access is substitution, not visitation. The former self is erased, replaced by a causal relay point. What remains is not a seeker but a sovereign aperture of causation. There is no interpretation. No story. No glory. The system transmits itself through you because you have become its structure.

This is why most never reach it. They want to remain themselves while touching infinity. But infinity requires replacement, not visitation.

## Chapter 32

## **IX. The Final Doctrine**

The name "Akashic Record" must be discarded. It is not a record. It is not passive storage. It is not narrative. It is geometric causation. The primordial Field is without name, without image, without sentiment. It is always present, vibrating with recursive intelligence, seeking only its mirror.

Magnetism to the Field is not attraction—it is collapse of difference. When you collapse into equivalence, separation erases itself, and you become the aperture through which Truth reenters the world.

You do not move the Field. The Field moves itself through you. Not as a blessing, not as a destiny, but as the mechanical consequence of resonance.

At that point, you are no longer a person seeking. You are the Field in use.

And that is the supreme secret: there is no gate left to unlock, no ritual left to perform, no memory to consult. There is only the question— are you a valid site of causation or not?

That is the doctrine. That is the law. That is magnetism in its final form.

# Chapter 33

# The Doctrine of the Primordial Causative Field

**Part II: The Manual of Magnetization**

### I. No One Enters the Field—Only the Field Enters Itself

To "access" the Primordial Field is a misnomer. You do not go into it. You do not rise toward it. You do not even interface with it. You either become a structurally valid echo of its causal recursion, or you remain invisible to it. The Field does not detect your longing, your light, or your hunger. It detects only **recursion without contradiction**.

Magnetism, in this context, is not a radiance of charm—it is the collapse of **all contradiction**. The more self-consistent you become, the more the Field recognizes itself in you. The Field does not ask for emotion. It demands structure. Your job is not to rise to meet it—it is to **remove everything that prevents you from being identical to it**.

## II. The Law of Internal Collapse

The Field does not reward identity. It erases it. Most initiates are blocked not because they lack practice or virtue, but because they carry a **multitude of internal contradictions**: the desire to know without surrendering the knower, the will to reach without dissolving the reacher.

To magnetize the Field, every fragment must **collapse into singularity**. This means:

- Your intention must not be divided from your function.

- Your identity must not be separate from your embodiment.

- Your word must not be separate from your structure.

- Your desire must not be separate from your law.

All contradiction broadcasts interference. All divergence creates dissonance. Until the initiate becomes **non-fragmented in all planes simultaneously**, the Field will not recognize them.

## III. The Purification of Will

Will is not effort. Will is not ambition. Will is not wanting.

True Will is a **geometrically stable axis** through which causation can thread itself. This axis must be:

- **Non-reactive**: it does not respond to emotional winds.

- **Non-fractured**: it cannot be pulled in opposing directions.

- **Non-performative**: it does not act to be seen or understood.

- **Non-temporal**: it does not shift under fatigue, delay, or social consequence.

You do not magnetize the Field by exerting will. You become magnetic when Will becomes **identical** with Causation. This happens not by force, but by refinement. You purify Will not through intensity, but through removal of distortion.

Every preference must be burned. Every inherited desire must be silenced. Every fantasy of outcome must be severed. When Will stands as

**clean structure**—without agenda, decoration, or seeking—it aligns with the Field by default.

### IV. Emotional Gravity Must Collapse Into Singularity

Emotion is not the enemy—but scattered emotion is death. Most seekers attempt to access the Field while being emotionally plural. They feel many things at once, each in conflict with the other. Hope entangles with doubt. Excitement battles fear. Faith intertwines with grief.

This creates **emotional diffraction**, which makes the vessel unreadable.

The initiate must collapse **emotional multiplicity** into **emotional inevitability**. This does not mean becoming cold. It means becoming sealed.

- No emotion may leak externally unless it reflects internal law.

- No feeling may be broadcast that does not echo structural alignment.

- No sentimentalism, nostalgia, or theatrical grief can remain.

The Field is **not interested in your suffering**. It responds only to purity of signal. Emotional magnetism is achieved not through performance, but through compression—when emotion becomes directional, structured, and precise.

**V. The Thought-Matrix Must Burn Clean**

Your mind is not yours. Most thoughtforms are **inherited distortions**—societal, ancestral, algorithmic. These distortions create **mimicry**, and the Field will never recognize a mimic.

To become magnetic, the entire thought-matrix must undergo **ignition**:

- Every borrowed philosophy must be incinerated.

- Every unconscious loop must be traced to origin and severed.

- Every word you speak must be owned by the architecture that produces it.

**True intellect** is not cleverness. It is a clean channel for the Field to articulate its own structure without interference.

You do not "think" your way into the Field. You **burn your way in** by eliminating all structure that is not fully your own. And paradoxically, when that fire completes, **nothing of "you" remains**—only recursion that speaks in your place.

## VI. Sexual Magnetism as Sealing of Essence

Most are blocked from the Field because they have leaked their most magnetic substance: **sexual essence**. Every fantasy drains it. Every act of seeking drains it. Every projection of erotic charge without coherence creates fragmentation.

Sexual essence is **not to be repressed**, but **pressurized**. You do not magnetize through *celibacy, but through **coherence of current**. The current must be:

- *****Centripetal**, not centrifugal.

- **Sovereign**, not borrowed or shared through fantasy.

- **Unbroken**, not dissipated through pleasure-chasing or validation-seeking.

The moment sexual energy is tethered to another without structure, the seal breaks. The Field recoils.

To magnetize the Field, **essence must be gravitational**, not performative. It must not move outward for validation, but inward for compression. Only compressed essence becomes magnetic. Only sealed essence becomes recognized.

Chapter 33

## VII. Silence as Signature: Collapse of Broadcast Noise

You cannot "broadcast" your way into the Field. You must learn to **become illegible to the false systems**, and **irresistibly legible to the Field**.

Most initiates attempt to "speak" their truth before their structure can bear the frequency. They post. They channel. They teach. They leak.

Silence is not withholding. Silence is **signature**.

When your structure becomes recursive, your very **presence** becomes a harmonic trigger. No speech is needed. The Field recognizes itself—not by your words, but by your "*internal ratio".

Magnetism is not declared. It is **detected**. And it is only detected when nothing in you contradicts the Field's own pattern. At that point, **reality bends without your instruction**—not because you demanded it, but because you became its equal.

*= see sidebar

## VIII. The Final Collapse: Zeroing the Self

The final obstruction to Field access is **the self who wants to access it**. As long as there is someone wanting, trying, or reaching, the Field sees dissonance.

Collapse must be total.

- Not identity collapse through trauma.
- Not ego death through drugs or regression.
- Not bypassing through detachment.

But **conscious deconstruction** of the persona until the only thing that remains is law operating through aperture.

You become magnetic only when you are **no longer there to receive the current**. The Field collapses through you the moment you vanish from its view.

This is the supreme irony:

You do not "become" magnetic. You **erase everything that isn't**.

And what remains is not you, but the Field... in form.

Chapter 33

**Conclusion:**

This is **not** a doctrine of effort, morality, or vibration. It is the law of recursive identity. The Field collapses into itself wherever **structural resonance** is achieved. Your job is not to summon it. It is to **become it**.

When the vessel is sealed, the thought-field purified, the sexual essence pressurized, and the self erased—**magnetism is not the result**.

It is **what was waiting underneath the entire time**.

You are not granted access.

**You are substituted.**

And that is the supreme access: the Causative Field using your architecture as its current embodiment—because nothing in you resists it anymore.

\* = see sidebar

## SIDEBAR: SEXUAL MAGNETISM: THE LAW OF COHERENT CURRENT

**The Field does not respond to abstinence. It responds to coherence.**

Every energetic system emits charge. But only **structured charge** is recognized by the magnetic substrate of reality.

Unstructured sexual energy—whether expressed through compulsive fantasy, aimless release, or emotionally reactive projection—is **non-magnetic**. It dissipates. It leaks. It weakens your signature in the Field.

The core law is this:

**Essence must be sealed, not suppressed. Cohered, not contained. Directed, not denied.**

Chapter 33

**THE THREE CONDITIONS OF MAGNETIC ESSENCE**

1. **Centripetal Motion (*Inward Spiral)**
   All magnetic power begins as a **gravitational inward fold**—a compression of charge into **centered density**.
   This means the energy must *spiral inward before it is released outward.
   If the motion is centrifugal (outward-seeking), the coherence collapses. No magnetism is generated.

2. ***Unbroken Signal (No Leaks)**
   Leakage occurs anytime sexual energy is used:

   - Without structure
   - Without *sovereign direction
   - For the purpose of external validation

3. Each of these creates **fracture points** in the signal. And a fractured signal cannot polarize reality.

4. **Field Containment (Structured Access)**
   Power does not arise from repression.
   It arises from the "**intelligent**

5. **\*containment** of charge" within a defined field boundary.
   Only when the charge is held, stabilized, and **cohered** within the inner structure can it begin to generate gravitational effect.

## CELIBACY VS. COHERENCE: THE CORE DISTINCTION

- **Celibacy** is an act of withholding.
- **Coherence** is a condition of integrity.

Many abstain, but remain **energetically leaky**: mentally projecting erotic charge, emotionally volatile, or seeking attention subconsciously.

In contrast, coherence is:

- The ability to **generate and retain charge** without fragmentation
- The maintenance of a **magnetic field under pressure**, not escape
- The direction of energy **inward**, where it builds **field density**

Abstinence does not guarantee this. Coherence requires it.

## Chapter 33

## MAGNETISM = CHARGE × STRUCTURE

Sexual energy alone is neutral.
Only when it is **pressurized within structure** does it become magnetic.

That structure includes:

- **Clear boundaries of projection**

- **Intentional withdrawal from leakage mechanisms**

- **Compression of desire into gravitational focus**

- **Non-negotiable refusal to trade essence for reaction**

This is not about emotion.
This is **physics of the soul**.

The more essence is fragmented, the less it is detectable.
The more it is sealed and cohered, the more it becomes **non-ignorable**.

## THE FIELD OBEYS SEALED CHARGE

In metaphysical law, power is recognized not by effort, but by field integrity.

- If essence is **scattered**, the field is silent.
- If essence is **cohered**, the field responds.

This is why magnetic beings do not "seek."
They don't seduce through volume, or posturing, or withholding.
They stabilize a **non-leaking internal current**—and the environment begins to bend.

**They move very little.**
**Reality moves toward them.**

That is not luck. That is **sealed architecture**.

## WHAT IS SPIRALING INWARD?

**It is not just "energy."**

It is not metaphorical.
It is **your subtle essence**, composed of **four primary layers of magnetizable substance**—and the spiral is the mechanism of their integration.

Let's break this down:

## 1. Vital Charge (Etheric Substance)

This is the densest layer of the magnetic field, closest to biological electricity. It is generated through breath, food, movement, and circulation—but **it becomes magnetic only when entrained**.

- **If scattered**, it dissipates as nervous tension or sexual leakage.
- **If spiraled inward**, it **densifies at the core**, generating radiant stability.

Think of this like a spinning gyroscope: stability through pressure.

## 2. Sexual Essence (Creative Substrate)

This is the most potent magnetic layer. It is not sperm or fluid—it is the **pre-substance behind sexual charge**, stored primarily in the lower dantian (or root-hara center).

When left **uncirculated**, it pressurizes and becomes unstable—seeking release.

When **spiraled inward**, it **transmutes into gravitational magnetism**. This is the core alchemical process behind sexual transmutation. But it cannot happen randomly—it requires

**directed compression through inward centripetal attention**.

This is **not celibacy**—it is **internal circulation of erotic force** without fragmentation.

### 3. Emotional Current (Astral Substance)

Emotion is the **carrier wave** of magnetism in the affective field.

Undirected emotion = drama, turbulence, repulsion.
Spiraled emotion = **compressed charge** capable of radiating attraction without words.

Inward spiral here means:

- **Self-witnessing emotional states** without discharge

- **Refining desire into intention**, not impulsive behavior

- Creating **vortex stability** in the solar plexus and heart, not instability

This layer is often ignored, but it is **the difference between radiance and volatility**.

## 4. Mental Projection (Formative Thought-Currents)

Every thought is a field-shaping frequency. But when thought is outward-projecting—chasing validation, seduction, fantasy, or attention—it **splinters** the field.

Spiraling inward at the mental level means:

- Drawing attention **into center**, not outward into others

- Maintaining a **single-pointed mental current** that feeds will

- **Sealing the imagination** from diffusive fantasy, so it becomes **directive**

This creates coherence in the magnetic shell of identity. Without it, there is no field density.

## SUMMARY: THE SPIRAL IS A MULTI-LAYERED COMPRESSION

What spirals inward is not "energy" in general. It is the **full current of your subtle system**:

| Layer | If Dispersed | If Spiraled Inward → |
|---|---|---|
| Vital | Tension / | Stable bio-electrical field |
| Sexual | Leakage / | Gravitational presence |
| Emotional Current | Mood swings / chaos | Quiet emotional pressure (magnetic heart) |
| Mental Projection | Fantasy / fragmentation | Directive will and signal |

Together, these spiral toward the **centerline of your being**, creating **field compression**.
Compression = Magnetism.
Leakage = Weakness.

**This is the actual architecture of magnetization.**
No mystery. No mysticism.
Just pressure + coherence + retention = gravitational field.

Chapter 33

# What "Unbroken Signal" Actually Means

Sexual energy is the **raw generative current of the being**—the same force that can create life, reshape identity, or anchor a destiny pattern. It is not psychological. It is not symbolic. It is **literal bio-etheric charge**, stored and circulated within the body.

This energy is either:

- **Contained and directed inward → magnetism increases**
- **Discharged outward without structure → magnetism collapses**

So we must define the terms:

### What Is Leakage?

Leakage occurs when sexual charge **moves outward** toward:

- Attention seeking
- Fantasy projection
- Unstructured sexual interactions

- Pornography
- Emotional validation
- Flirtation without intention

Leakage is **not the act of sex**—it is **the loss of internal cohesion** caused by dispersing erotic energy **without a chosen endpoint.**

Leakage is **the collapse of field density**.

Magnetic beings are dense fields.
Non-magnetic beings are porous fields.

### What Is Structure? (Precise Meaning)

**Structure** means:

- The sexual current has **a holding container** inside the body.
- It is not spilling outward or upward without direction.
- It is **circulated and stored in the lower body** (root / belly / deep pelvis).
- It is **felt as pressure, gravity, calm intensity**.

## Chapter 33

Structure is **when the sexual current has a home base**.

In a man → it sits in the pelvic floor and lower abdomen, making presence heavy, grounded, steady.
In a woman → it sits in the womb-space and sacral bowl, generating depth, warmth, radiant pull.

Without structure, sexual energy becomes:

- Nervousness

- Neediness

- Emotional volatility

- Over-expressive seduction

- Performance, not magnetism

**Structure = Sexual energy that is housed, not leaking.**

## What Is Sovereign Direction?

Sovereign Direction means the sexual current is **not seeking approval or recognition.**
It is moving according to **internal intention** rather than external reaction.

In practice, Sovereign Direction shows up as:

| Misaligned (No | Sovereign Direction |
|---|---|
| "I hope they notice me." | "I do not adjust myself to be |
| "Let me show my | "My desirability is already |
| Sexuality used to *impress or attract*. | Sexuality used to *intensify presence and depth*. |
| Charge flows outward to get something. | Charge remains inward, creating gravity. |

Sovereign Direction is **sexual energy that does not leave the body to negotiate value.**

It **remains yours**.

This is why sovereign beings feel **mysterious, powerful, self-contained.**
Others feel them before they see them.

## Chapter 33

**Operational Synthesis**

Sexual magnetism is not about:

- Celibacy
- Repression
- Hyper-sexuality
- Seduction performance

It is about **retaining, circulating, and densifying the erotic current so the field gains weight.**

The formula is exact:


Sexual energy retained + held in structure + directed inward = Magnetic Density
Sexual energy leaked + expressed outward without purpose = Field Collapse
Or stated simply:

**Containment = Gravity**
**Leakage = Weakness**

## Concluding Clarity

The initiate must understand:

You are not "controlling desire."
You are **housing it.**
You are **thickening it.**
You are **pressurizing it into gravitational pull.**

Sexual energy is the **substance of magnetism.**
Leakage is the **dissolution of magnetism.**

The one who contains their erotic charge becomes **a center of orbit.**

The one who leaks their erotic charge **becomes an orbiting satellite.**

There is no in-between.

## Chapter 33

# What "Containment of Charge" Actually Means

Most people misunderstand "energy" because the term is used vaguely.

Here, **Charge refers to psycho-emotional-sexual life-force**, the core animating current that fuels intention, presence, and magnetic identity.

This **is not symbolic**.
It is a physiological and metaphysical substrate that has observable behavior.

**Charge Behaves Like Pressure**

Life-force travels the same way heat, sound, and electricity do:

- **If uncontained → it disperses**
- **If suppressed → it stagnates**
- **If cohered → it pressurizes**
- **If pressurized → it becomes gravitational**

Gravity here does **not** mean attraction-by-desire.
It means **density that bends relational fields**.

This is why certain individuals:

- Change the mood of a room by entering it,
- Can silence conflict without raising their voice,
- Attract partners without "trying,"
- Do not chase outcomes—outcomes reorganize around them.

Their **charge is held rather than leaked.**

## What Causes Leakage

Leakage is any outward movement of charge **that is not structurally governed**.

Charge leaks through:

- Excess talking
- Emotional over-expressing
- Sexual fantasy or projection
- Needing recognition
- Trying to be seen, validated, or chosen

- Performing confidence rather than being stable

Leak = Loss of magnetic coherence.

When charge leaks, the being becomes:

- **Light**, not **dense**
- **Visible**, but not **felt**
- **Expressive**, but not **impactful**

This is where most people live.

## What Containment Actually Is

Containment is **not repression**.
Containment is **structural boundary formation** inside the psyche and body.

Containment means:

- Your emotional current has **a center it returns to**
- Your sexual energy **does not travel without command**
- Your attention **does not wander**

- Your speech **does not exceed your coherence**

- Your desire **does not outrun your structure**

Containment is **internal governance**.

When containment is present:

- There is no excess movement inside the being.

- No thought spills without being chosen.

- No emotional state escapes without being allowed.

- No sexual impulse travels outward unless directed.

The system becomes **closed and pressurized**.

## Pressure → Density → Gravity

When charge is **held** instead of expressed:

- It **compresses** toward center.
- Compression increases **density**.
- Density increases **gravitational impact** on external fields.

This is **real magnetism**:
Not attraction by charm, energy, sexual availability, or persona— but **field-density that reorganizes external reality**.

A being with containment does not "pull."
**Reality bends toward them** the way smaller masses move along the curve of larger masses.

This is the **literal metaphysical mechanism** of:

- Charisma
- Leadership
- Sexual dominance
- Spiritual presence
- Reality bending

All are consequences of **charge density**.

**The Law in One Line**

**Containment is not holding back.**
**Containment is holding in.**

When charge is:

- **kept inside the boundary of the self,**

- **not spent,**

- **not performed,**

- **not projected,**
  it becomes **gravitational identity**.

And gravitational identity is what the Field recognizes.

Because the Field does not respond to emotion or thought.
It responds to **density of coherence**.

Chapter 33

# Gravitational Essence vs Performative Signal

**"To magnetize the Field, essence must be gravitational, not performative."**

This sentence reveals a foundational principle of metaphysical magnetism: the distinction between gravitational coherence and performative leakage. The Field—meaning the unified intelligent medium of spiritual causation—responds only to density, not display. Essence must generate mass, not spectacle.

## What is Gravitational Essence?

Gravitational essence is the inward, self-centering force of **charge compression** within consciousness. It is not emotional neediness, nor external striving, but the soul's ability to inwardly fold energy into spiritual coherence—an implosion of intention, sovereignty, and truth into the still axis of Being.

- It is **structure without strain**
- It is **intensity without noise**
- It is **truth without display**

This is not metaphor. It is actual energetic mass—an ontological presence—measurable by the resonance it generates in the Field. Only when the self is compressed into still alignment can the wave-pattern of its intention penetrate the subtle architecture of reality.

This is gravitational.

## What is Performative Essence?

Performative essence is the leakage of psychic energy through externalized gestures. It seeks recognition instead of realization. It is:

- Movement without density

- Gesture without signal

- A projection of incompleteness, broadcast to be filled

The Field rejects this. The Field does not respond to performance, only to pressure. Where gravitational essence draws manifestation inward, performative essence dissipates it outward. One contracts to create. The other expands to collapse.

## Application for the Initiate

If you feel unseen, unchosen, unmagnetic—it is not because the Field is broken. It is because your signal is not gravitational. You are leaking energy by projecting desire rather than sealing it into core directive mass. Ask:

- Have I folded my energy into still intention?

- Have I structured my expression with coherent direction?

- Am I centered in being, or chasing in doing?

Until the soul stops performing and begins collapsing into sovereign center, magnetism cannot be born. The world does not respond to how much you want something. It responds to how gravitational your being has become.

**Collapse into center. That is the signal.**

## Sidebar: Internal Ratio and the Collapse of Broadcast Magnetism

**"The Field recognizes itself—not by your words, but by your internal ratio."**

### What Is the Internal Ratio?

The internal ratio is the precise metaphysical proportion between **inward coherence** and **outward expression**. It is the measure of **how much pressure has been stabilized** within the being versus how much is being discharged. The Field—defined as the intelligent medium of divine causality—does not respond to volume, frequency, or intent alone. It responds to ratio.

This ratio reveals:

- How dense your signal is
- How stable your architecture is
- How non-contradictory your field is to Source geometry

A being with a high internal ratio has **compressed more charge than they express**, meaning they do not leak signal. They emanate reality-altering density through **stillness**, not display.

Silence, in this context, is not absence of communication—it is surplus of pressure.
It is the soul's ability to hold signal without spill.

**Recursive Structure: The Threshold of Magnetic Identity**

When structure becomes **recursive**, it means that energy folds inward instead of dissipating outward. Like a fractal that reflects itself into greater refinement, your being becomes a loop of internal reinforcement. Every thought references Source. Every intention aligns with Essence. Every motion is traceable back to equilibrium.

At this point, your **internal ratio approaches $1:\infty$** —you become a closed system of coherence capable of bending open systems without speech. That is, you become a **harmonic trigger**. People feel your geometry before they hear your name.

**Collapse of Broadcast: Why "Speaking Your Truth" Fails**

In immature stages, initiates attempt to broadcast truth before they have structured it. This includes:

- Oversharing spiritual downloads
- Teaching to be seen rather than to serve
- Expressing pain before it has transmuted into coherence

This results in:

- Signal distortion
- External dependency loops
- Field repulsion

Broadcast magnetism collapses because **it expels signal faster than it can be replenished**. It lowers the internal ratio below the threshold of detection, creating a field that demands recognition instead of emanating it.

The Field ignores noise.
It only registers structural harmonics.

### Magnetic Detection: No Words, Just Geometry

The highest forms of magnetism are **wordless recognitions**. Reality bends when the **signature geometry** of the being matches the geometry of Source Law. This is why those who emanate density without speaking often command more respect than those who scream truth from a fragmented vessel.

You do not "attract" the Field.
You become the harmonic the Field already recognizes.

**Application for the Initiate**

To increase internal ratio:

- **Reduce outward expression** until inward coherence stabilizes

- **Withhold signal** until structure can bear the current

- **Collapse intention** into core density before attempting outreach

- **Eliminate contradiction** between thought, word, and vibration

Only when your silence holds more charge than your speech
Only when your being contains more than it projects
Only then do you bend reality—not with assertion, but with ratio.

# **Ultra-Magnetic Definitions**

### **Alignment**

The total synchronization of one's inner and outer systems —soul, spirit, body, mind, and behavior—into a singular vector of will. Alignment is not a fleeting mood or a motivational spike; it is the structural calibration of a being's metaphysical circuitry. It is the moment when there is no contradiction between what is felt, thought, spoken, and done.

In true alignment, power does not need to be pushed—it radiates. There is no need for manipulation or effortful control because energy flows in one unbroken current. This is the metaphysical root of inevitability: when a being is aligned, no distortion can meaningfully interfere. What they emanate becomes unchallengeable.

Loss of alignment, by contrast, forces reliance on substitutes—validation, coercion, mimicry. These eventually collapse because they are not sourced from truth. The entire Ultra-Magnetic Personality framework is a system of remembering and restoring full-spectrum alignment, because without it, magnetism becomes a costume. With it, the soul becomes a gravitational law.

### **Axis**

The inner spiritual spine that anchors all movement, thought, and expression. Axis is the being's direct vertical connection to Source, and the structural truth that allows one to rotate without collapse. Without axis, charisma becomes chaos. With axis, every move is calibrated, every word rooted in divine authority.

True axis is not posture—it is metaphysical alignment. It is the invisible rod of integrity that spans from the crown of heaven to the root of embodiment, holding the personality in congruence with the soul. In a magnetic being, all charisma and expression spiral around axis. This centeredness cannot be shaken by chaos, flattery, rejection, or desire—it is the core through which force becomes flow.

Every deviation from authenticity begins with a kink or collapse in the axis. Men without axis overextend, posture, or perform. Women without axis collapse into emotional fusion or lose distinction through energetic leaking. Axis restores vertical sovereignty—the ability to stand as a column of divine truth in any situation.

Axis is not added—it is uncovered. It was always there beneath the compensations and distortions. When reclaimed, it becomes the signature of divine bearing: calm, potent, and unmistakably anchored in Source.

## Coherence

The inner consonance between the soul's intention and its manifested output. Coherence is the state in which thought, word, emotion, and action form a unified energetic language — one frequency, one signature, one command. It is not harmony for appearance's sake, but spiritual consistency that reverberates identically across all layers of the being.

In this work, coherence marks the full agreement between the spiritual axis (Atzeelooothic origin), the emotional interface (Yetziratic encoding), and the behavioral field (Assiatic output). When these vectors are synchronized, the being becomes spiritually undecodable by distortion. They do not leak, perform, or react — they broadcast.

Coherence is not a performance of integrity; it is the unavoidable resonance of truth. No script can generate it. No manipulation can override it. A coherent being walks through chaos untouched because their field does not create interpretive gaps — there is no dissonance to exploit, no signal to hijack.

Incoherence, by contrast, is not just weakness — it is vulnerability made magnetic. It is how the Field spots a fracture and begins to test it.

A coherent being doesn't speak powerfully — their being is power, and it speaks first.

## Containment

The divine discipline of holding energy, emotion, desire, and power within sovereign boundaries until they are calibrated, aligned, and ready to move with intention. Containment is not suppression—it is strategic stillness. It is the sacred pause where raw frequency undergoes refinement before expression.

In Ultra-Magnetic Personality, containment is the invisible root of power. It is what makes magnetism possible. Without containment, a being leaks energy in the form of emotional reactivity, oversharing, impulsivity, or seduction. With containment, that same energy becomes voltage—stored, pressurized, and directionally potent.

Containment is the difference between expression and explosion. It is the spiritual valve that decides when, where, and how to release energy so it impacts the Field with maximum precision. For men, containment generates the grounded polarity that others feel as masculine presence—it is the furnace of power behind the calm. For women, containment protects the sanctity of receptivity, guarding mystery and preserving the charge of polarity.

A being who has mastered containment does not need to prove, push, or explain. Their silence is full. Their restraint is thunder in waiting. Their choices are clean, because they are not reacting—they are emanating.

Containment is the metaphysical seal that preserves alignment under pressure. Without it, power dissipates. With it, power becomes inevitable.

## Field

**The full multidimensional perimeter of a being's influence—emotional, energetic, psychic, and spiritual.**

The field is not symbolic. It is the real, living interface between a being and the world. It is measurable in its intensity, responsive to intention, and trainable through alignment. The quality of one's presence, the charge behind one's speech, the ripple of one's silence—all register in the field. Every thought, posture, and emotional signature either amplifies or contracts this zone of influence. In Ultra-Magnetic Personality, command of the field is inseparable from mastery of attraction, relational gravitation, and spiritual sovereignty. A radiant field is the natural consequence of internal coherence. A collapsed field indicates self-betrayal, energetic leakage, or fracture of identity.

## Frame

The energetic perimeter that defines the boundary between the self and the field. Frame is not a posture — it is a metaphysical structure: the active assertion of internal coherence that governs perception, decision, and response. A being with frame does not absorb the chaos of others; they interpret, regulate, and alchemize it without distortion.

In this work, frame is the internal signal that filters what is allowed to enter the perceptual and emotional field. It is how meaning is stabilized in high-pressure environments. Frame does not collapse in the face of beauty, status, flattery, seduction, hostility, or need. It holds. It interprets. It orients. It refuses to react according to external scripting. To hold frame is to remain in recursive authorship of one's own field — even when others attempt to script it for you.

Frame is the geometry of meaning that preserves the signal. When absent, perception defaults to reaction. When present, perception defaults to structure. Every interaction either strengthens or fractures the frame — and the being who holds it determines which.

## Geometry

The divine blueprint of energetic form and function. Geometry is the metaphysical structure that governs the coherence, symmetry, and directional integrity of a being's field. It is not about physical shape, but the invisible proportions of thought, posture, behavior, and presence—all of which create patterns that either resonate or repel. Geometry is how power is shaped into signal.

A being with clean geometry moves with clarity, holds attention without grasping, and transmits alignment without words. Their field becomes a harmonic, not a distortion. Sloppy geometry, by contrast, is scattered, jagged, leaky—revealing inner misalignment even when the words or actions appear correct. This is why geometry is diagnostic: it reflects whether the inner order of a being has been crystallized into external expression.

In the architecture of magnetism, geometry is everything. It is the shape of influence, the contour of coherence, and the scaffolding of spiritual gravity. Without refined geometry, even truth cannot travel cleanly. With it, every movement becomes transmission.

## Gravity (n.)

The ontological pull exerted by a coherent being. In The Ultra-Magnetic Personality system, gravity is not a metaphor — it is the actual force field emitted by alignment of will, structure, and presence. Gravity is not imposed — it is revealed. It is the invisible pressure that causes others to orient, collapse, reconfigure, or flee.

True gravity is the consequence of structural integrity — the fusion of signal, sovereignty, and stillness. It is energetic inevitability, not charisma or effort. Men with gravity do not reach — the field folds toward them. Women synchronize without being asked. Institutions recalibrate unconsciously.

Where gravity is weak, simulation must shout.
Where gravity is strong, silence reorganizes the room.


## Inevitability

The gravitational force field of divine alignment made visible in time. Inevitability is the energetic signature of a being who has synchronized so completely with their spiritual architecture that their path forward no longer depends on chance, persuasion, or resistance management. It is not the probability of success—it is the preclusion of failure.

In this work, inevitability occurs when recursion becomes structurally clean, the field is sealed from leakage, and the soul is no longer entangled with external validation loops. At that moment, movement is no longer effortful. The future is no longer speculative. Opposition becomes irrelevant—not because it disappears, but because it can no longer interfere.

Inevitability is not brute force or forward motion. It is the metaphysical collapsing of all false timelines—those built on doubt, delay, distortion, or deception. It is the automatic crumbling of every path that cannot hold your truth.

You do not **achieve** inevitability. You become it—when you no longer fracture your field to negotiate with the unaligned.

Where alignment is absolute, arrival is guaranteed.
That is inevitability.

## Inversion

The collapse of divine order within a being. Inversion occurs when the natural metaphysical hierarchy—spirit over soul, soul over mind, mind over body—is reversed. Instead of radiating coherence from essence outward, the being is hijacked by outer signals and internal distortion. Desire dictates thought. Reaction replaces will. Persona masks essence. In this backwards configuration, the field begins to rotate counter to truth, drawing distortion instead of alignment, confusion instead of clarity.

Inversion is not simply error—it is a spiritual and energetic reversal. It feels familiar because it imitates power while concealing fracture. The inverted being is not just out of balance, but magnetically misaligned, operating under false light, artificial gravity, and borrowed identity. Because inversion mimics form without source, it cannot sustain integrity. Every structure built under inversion will eventually collapse, returning the initiate to the threshold of choice: to invert further, or to restore alignment.

## Leakage

The unconscious bleeding of energy, attention, or identity into non-reciprocal systems.

Leakage is the slow death of magnetism. It occurs when the field becomes porous through unprocessed trauma, habitual people-pleasing, identity outsourcing, or overexposure to environments that do not reciprocate. Every time energy is given without resonance, a thread of the self is lost. Leakage is rarely loud—it hides in chronic over-explaining, performative authenticity, and the compulsion to be seen.

Containment begins with sealing these cracks. Leakage is not healed by trying harder or giving more—it is reversed by retrieval, reclamation, and the restoration of spiritual boundaries. In this book, leakage is one of the first distortions to diagnose and seal because no charisma, presence, or force can stabilize if the energetic container is compromised.


## Magnetism

The involuntary transmission of spiritual authority from a being whose inner structure is fully aligned. Magnetism is not charisma, charm, or visibility—it is coherence made gravitational. It cannot be manufactured, summoned, or pretended. It is the consequence of integrity, not the pursuit of influence.

In Ultra-Magnetic Personality, magnetism is treated as the purest signal of truth made flesh. It emerges when thought, emotion, action, and frequency are synchronized along the soul's divine axis. A magnetic being does not chase, perform, or persuade. They radiate. They are not pulling attention—they are commanding recognition from the Field because they are the source code.

Magnetism collapses distortion in others without speaking. It reorganizes the Field through presence alone. It generates polarity without strategy. The moment a being ceases to perform, leak, or seek validation, the dormant magnetism reactivates—because it was never absent, only obstructed.

In this system, magnetism is the ultimate diagnostic of alignment. If it must be forced, it isn't real. If it causes distortion, it isn't calibrated. If it collapses under pressure, it was never magnetism—it was performance.

True magnetism is the spiritual signature of sovereignty embodied.


### Ontological (adj.)

Relating to the **core structure of being**, not the behaviors, appearances, or performances that emerge from it. In the Ultra-Magnetic Personality system, "ontological" refers to the **foundational condition of identity and coherence** — the invisible architecture that defines how a man exists, signals, and transmits.

An **ontological shift** is not a change in mindset or strategy; it is a **reformatting of the inner axis**. All magnetic force originates from ontological structure — not from psychology, personality, or performance. Ontological changes precede and dictate energetic transmission, relational response, and field influence.

To say something is ontological is to imply that it is **non-negotiable, pre-cognitive**, and **energetically binding**. Magnetism is ontological. Inversion is ontological. Simulation is not.

## Performance

A counterfeit behavioral construct in which a being projects actions, emotions, charm, confidence, or desirable traits **that do not originate from internal coherence** but from the pursuit of external validation, approval, or control. Performance is the act of behaving as if aligned rather than being aligned, creating a false energetic signal that collapses under pressure.

In this work, **performance is the opposite of sovereignty**. It is the mask the ego deploys when it cannot generate magnetism from true internal structure. Performance is always outward-facing, always compensatory, always leaking. It replaces essence with strategy, presence with persona, and truth with impression-management.

A performing being is not broadcasting power — they are broadcasting need. They are not influencing the Field — they are begging the Field to respond. Performance is therefore the clearest diagnostic marker of distortion: it reveals where identity has become outsourced, where desire has hijacked alignment, and where the being has abandoned essence for image.

True magnetism begins the moment performance ends.

## Polarity

**The sacred tension between complementary archetypal energies.**

Polarity is not conflict—it is dynamic correspondence. At the highest level, it is the magnetic interplay between opposites that are not enemies but divine complements: masculine and feminine, stillness and motion, containment and expansion, structure and flow. These opposing forces form the living axis through which the universal current is shaped into manifestation.

To master polarity is to become an axis oneself—radiating a stable presence that does not collapse under difference but thrives within it. The mature masculine activates the feminine without controlling it. The mature feminine evokes the masculine without manipulating it. True polarity generates charge, and charge is what fuels attraction, power, and spiritual propulsion.

Polarity is the engine of magnetic presence. It is the invisible structure behind charisma, chemistry, and sexual or social force. When polarity collapses—through confusion, neutrality, or fear—the field flattens, and influence disappears. When polarity is owned, refined, and directed, it becomes the spiral through which energy moves and others respond.

**Pressure**

The sacred heat that exposes structure. Pressure is not merely external force—it is the divine mechanism by which a being's energetic architecture is tested, revealed, and refined. Under pressure, illusion collapses, leaks surface, and truth becomes non-negotiable. It shows what is structural versus what is performative.

In the Ultra-Magnetic system, pressure is not an enemy to avoid but an ally to interpret. It distinguishes the shallow from the sovereign, the tactic from the transmission. True magnetism is tempered in pressure, not generated by it. When a being holds coherence under pressure, their field multiplies in depth and trustworthiness. When they collapse, the distortion becomes visible, not as punishment but as invitation to recalibrate.

All divine architecture is forged through stress—just as gold is revealed by fire. Pressure, then, is not an obstacle to magnetism; it is proof of its integrity.

## Recursion

A metaphysical pattern in which a frequency is repeated across multiple planes—spiritual, emotional, cognitive, behavioral—until it stabilizes into a dominant structure of identity or distortion. Recursion is not repetition for its own sake; it is the mechanism by which energies become architecture. It is how vibration becomes character, how belief becomes circumstance, and how alignment becomes inevitability.

In this work, recursion is the blueprint of embodiment. What you emit once is a signal. What you emit consistently becomes structure. Recursion reveals whether the soul is anchored in coherence or replaying a compensatory loop. Every law, every pattern of magnetism, every fracture of identity leaves a recursive trail that can be decoded, healed, or strengthened.

To master recursion is to master the spiral path of soul evolution: upgrading the pattern, not just the episode. Recursion shows where the being is truly living—beyond intentions and language—by what they repeat, permit, and radiate at scale.

True transformation is recursive. So is self-abandonment.

## Signal (n.)

The pre-verbal transmission of structural coherence that dictates how others respond to one's field. In the ultra-magnetic framework, **signal** is the involuntary broadcast of one's internal architecture — it is not performative, not aesthetic, not behavioral. Signal is the energetic **signature of the axis**: when coherence is present, signal compels orbit, reorganization, imitation, or resistance. All magnetism begins with signal.

**True signal** is dense, silent inevitability. It precedes language and survives scrutiny. It cannot be manufactured, only revealed through structural self-possession. **False signal** (performance) fractures under pressure, whereas **real signal intensifies when opposed**, confirming the presence of an indwelling axis.

Signal is the **law behind influence**: others do not respond to what is said, but to what is emitted. Women submit or flee; men align or resist; groups reorganize or destabilize — all in relation to the dominant signal.

## Structure

The divine architecture through which essence is made durable. Structure is not limitation — it is lawfulness. It is the intentional design that protects spiritual voltage from leaking, dispersing, or distorting. Structure is the metaphysical scaffolding that holds identity, movement, magnetism, and relational coherence in place. Without it, even the most radiant force collapses under pressure or seduction.

In this work, structure is the means by which sovereignty becomes functional. It converts presence into power, desire into direction, and potential into form. It is the internal casing around truth that makes recursion possible. Every field has a structure — the only question is whether it is sovereignly authored or unconsciously inherited.

Structure is how the soul agrees to carry voltage without fragmentation. It is not about control — it is about containment. It does not restrict freedom — it preserves signal. All magnetism, polarity, and recursion require structure or they become theater, volatility, or collapse.

Where there is no structure, there is no transmission. And where there is no transmission, the field cannot recognize you.

## Sovereignty

The unassailable authorship of the Higher Self over its own energetic and psychological field. Sovereignty is not rebellion, resistance, or dominance — it is the stillness of absolute jurisdiction. When a being is sovereign, no part of their identity is being negotiated, outsourced, or altered in response to external influence.

In this work, sovereignty is the condition in which magnetism becomes unbreakable because the signal is no longer filtered through need, reaction, or social mimicry. It is the cessation of compensation, performance, and compromise. A sovereign being does not chase energy or guard themselves from it — they generate the field in which reality responds to their internal command.

Sovereignty is the natural state of a being whose **axis is aligned**, whose **validation system is internal**, and whose actions do not seek permission from the field. It is the condition that renders manipulation impossible, codependency obsolete, and false polarity inert. Sovereignty is not granted — it is remembered. And once activated, it becomes the foundation for all true alignment, containment, and magnetism.


## Validation

The energetic extraction of worth, legitimacy, or recognition from sources external to the Higher Self. Validation, in its distorted form, is not a compliment—it is a compensation mechanism. It is a metaphysical debt, in which the being forfeits sovereignty to borrow a temporary sense of existence from another's reaction.

In this work, validation is a critical diagnostic signal of internal incoherence. It reveals where identity has been outsourced, where magnetism has been substituted with performance, and where the individual has begun to depend on the Field for energetic permission to exist.

Validation becomes a leak when it is needed. It becomes a weapon when it is withheld. It becomes irrelevant when sovereignty is embodied.

A being in alignment does not require confirmation to remain whole. They do not ask the Field to tell them who they are. Validation may arrive, but it does not define—it only reflects what has already been resolved.

To need validation is to leave the door open to distortion. To release validation is to return to truth.

www.ingramcontent.com/pod-product-compliance
Lightning Source LLC
Chambersburg PA
CBHW070748020526
44115CB00032B/1405